Couvade Syndrome

What Male Sympathetic Pregnancy is

& how you can Fight it

By

P. A. Simon

Disclaimer

All the material contained in this book is provided for educational and informational purposes only. No responsibility can be taken for any results or outcomes resulting from the use of this material.

While every attempt has been made to provide information that is both accurate and effective, the author does not assume any responsibility for the accuracy or use/misuse of this information.

First edition: April 2020

ISBN 978-83-956837-3-2 (paperback)

ISBN 978-83-956837-4-9 (ebook)

Table of Contents

To my wife for her strength and perseverance.

To my beloved son for the joy and motivation, he gives.

Introduction

Pregnant mothers may likely experience a handful of symptoms such as morning sickness, nausea, anxiety, fatigue, body aches, and several others. But what's less known is the fact that soon-to-be fathers also experience several pregnancy symptoms too. So, if you feel that you're going crazy when you discover that as an expectant dad, you're having some of those symptoms your partner is having, then you shouldn't be anymore.

A study of 282 soon-to-be fathers was carried out by researchers at St. George's University, London. The age range of the men who were studied was between 19-55 years and during the pregnancy of all their partners, they attended St. George's hospital. The researchers compared their findings with a similar number of controls. In the course of the study period, the dads-to-be reported several symptoms such as depression, insomnia, toothache, back pain, mood swings, cramps, morning sickness, fainting and fatigue. In fact, there were extreme cases where some men had swollen stomachs similar to "baby bump." Interestingly, when 11 of the men in the study group complained about the symptoms they were having, there were no visible or physical causes. Well, most of these symptoms disappeared immediately after their wives delivered.

I guess this sounds interesting, right? Well, according to a senior lecturer at St George's who was also the leader of the study, Dr. Arthur Brennan, the soon-to-be dads were so attuned to their pregnant partners that they began to develop similar symptoms.

Is your wife pregnant? Have you ever heard that you look like someone who is set to deliver soon?

Do you find yourself experiencing morning sickness and you're wondering what the problem is? Has someone asked how many months you are or did people point to your stomach and ask you if you're expecting a boy or a girl? Well, most of the pregnancy symptoms along with the bulging belly doesn't imply that you've gone crazy. It's obvious that you're among the expectant men who may be experiencing a rare health issue known as Couvade Syndrome. Women are commonly seen as the only people who suffer the physical and psychological effects of pregnancy. Well, women are not actually the only ones being affected by pregnancy because it also affects male partners physiologically and psychologically.

You may not easily find a lot of research on couvade syndrome for several reasons. First, some daddies who may be experiencing the symptoms of the syndrome may not notice them. They may simply assume that this is just normal and in no way related to pregnancy at all. Well, if you've experienced certain changes in your body and you're wondering whether you're having symptoms of the syndrome, this is the right book you should be reading.

Are you already convinced that you're having symptoms of couvade syndrome? Never mind, you're not alone at all; there is a medical community backing you up. You will find useful tips and information shared later in this paper very helpful. Some readers may be interested in the topic simply because it's quite mysterious and gradually becoming common among expectant fathers. If you're in this category, then this is the perfect book you need to read to satisfy your curiosity. Get set to discover one of the strangest phenomena around the world. Enjoy reading!

Chapter I

Understanding Couvade Syndrome

Couvade Syndrome: What Exactly is it?

Generally, women are known to have several symptoms when they get pregnant. People see these symptoms and changes that women experience during pregnancy as normal and expected. But is it possible for men to also experience similar symptoms of pregnancy? Yes, of course. If you discover that as an expecting father, you're beginning to experience certain symptoms such as mood swings, bloating and weight gain, then it's most likely that you're having a condition known as *"couvade syndrome"* or sympathetic pregnancy.

There are different definitions of couvade syndrome; some of them focus mainly on the challenges associated with the syndrome's diagnosis, while others are medical. So, what exactly is couvade syndrome? Commonly experienced by men in industrialized societies around the world, the syndrome is derived from *"Couver"* which is a French term meaning to hatch, brood or nest.

Although it's challenging to obtain an accurate estimate of the frequency of the syndrome (mainly because the number of reports of individuals with the symptoms is low) it's a phenomenon that has recently begun to receive the attention of biologists around the world. The couvade syndrome is a condition experienced by men whose partners are pregnant and who start to experience symptoms of pregnancy. *It's important to note that for an expectant father to be regarded as having the couvade syndrome, then he must have been afflicted by at least two or more symptoms linked with couvade that are actually inexplicable.* There are several theories of the possible causes of the syndrome which isn't fully understood, but it has neither been identified as a mental or medical health issue. There are other names for this condition, such as male pregnancy experience, sympathetic pregnancy or pregnant dad syndrome. Apart from a wide range of definitions of what actually constitutes couvade syndrome, there is also a wide range of studies which estimates that the number of occurrences of the syndrome in expectant fathers within modern Western populations is between 20 and 80 percent.

Couvade Syndrome vs. Phantom Pregnancy

One of the mistakes people often make is to confuse sympathetic pregnancy with phantom pregnancy or a similar condition known as pseudopregnancy. Pseudopregnancy, which is also regarded as false pregnancy, is a clinical phenomenon found in non-pregnant females. Those who experience this false pregnant often exhibit different maternal behaviors as well as physical signs of pregnancy.

Experts are of the view that one possible cause of false pregnancy is the declining serum progesterone concentrations that are usually linked with the end of the luteal phase and this ends up leading to an increase in serum prolactin concentrations. Also, in the medical field, phantom pregnancy is seen as a mental health issue which is actually listed in the Diagnostic and Statistical Manual of Mental Disorders, fifth edition (DSM-5) as a somatic symptom disorder.

Phantom pregnancy is not a very common phenomenon, though Africa has more cases of the condition than other continents such as America and Europe. Women who have this condition believe that they are pregnant even when they're not. In fact, most of them exhibit several symptoms of pregnancy like:

- Feeling fetal movement
- Swollen breasts and stomach
- Labor pains especially at the estimated due date (However, the possibility of this happening is just 1 percent of all cases)
- Morning sickness
- Light periods and in some cases, no periods at all

Several reasons have been considered to be the cause of phantom pregnancy by researchers. For some cases, it may be as a result of a strong desire of a woman to become pregnant. Perhaps this is one good reason why it frequently occurs among couples who may be experiencing infertility issues. For other cases, it could be as a result of females having an intense fear of becoming pregnant while some studies suggest that it could even develop due to depression and its accompanying endocrine changes. Well, this is quite different from couvade syndrome and it only affects females. It shouldn't be confused with couvade syndrome.

Historical Evidence of Couvade Syndrome

Although most of the personal physical symptoms that we notice are relatively recent historical occurrences, sympathetic pregnancy has cultural precedence dating back several millennia. As explained by Dr. Frank L'Engle Williams, any kind of cultural behavior that attracts attention to the male and enables the male to be responsible for ensuring the survival of the infant is couvade syndrome. Such cultures don't just draw the attention of a father to the mother and child; it helps to inform the society that the father belongs to the child and the child belongs to the father.

A look at the hunter-gatherers on the Trobriand Island who lived off the coast of Papua New Guinea shows that they pass responsibility for a pregnancy to a dad figure by making use of the couvade ritual. Basically, the couvade ritual is often initiated partly to establish the expectant father (whether he is the biological father or not). Consequently, the father carries out multi-day simulations of birth pains in the course of the partner's pregnancy to showcase his connection to the laborer. It's not just empathetic to the pregnancy but also necessary and helps confirm to the group that he would be the father as well as the caretaker of the new baby. Well, you can still find such performative rituals in different locations around the world, but they are now a rare rite in modern times and exists in Africa, parts of the Caribbean and Asia. But what if our reaction to not having an outlet for ritualistic fatherhood is to experience some of the couvade symptoms such as swollen feet, nausea and several others? According to Williams, the strange twist from cultural to couvade ritual to the physical and biological manifestations of the syndrome may actually have evolutionary roots.

Ritualist Couvade Syndrome in Rural Societies

Even though couvade syndrome is often characterized by a male experiencing several symptoms of pregnancy involuntarily, ritualistic couvade, on the other hand, is a voluntary presentation of several social pregnancy behaviors. Also, ritualistic couvade is almost linked in a way to some rural societies while couvade syndrome is quite common among industrialized nations. Interestingly, there are several accounts of ritualistic couvade being reported around the world that are in several ways similar. The existence of couvade rituals was actually recorded way back 50 BC in Corsica and even among Iberians in Spain. The first time it was scientifically described was in the late 19th century when some anthropologists examined several customs that men performed which coincided with their partner's pregnancy. In 1929, Dawson proceeded to publish a primary collection of some accounts of couvade rituals around the world. In its basic form, the couvade ritual involves the man staying in his bed and feeling either imagined or real contractions as well as birth pains while his partner delivers their baby.

He also observed that the ritual assumes different forms which include a man disguising himself as his female partner and pretending to deliver a baby just like his partner does. In certain locations like the Black Carib of British Honduras, it was also recorded that in the 19th century, expectant fathers were required to go through a period of fasting along with severe restriction which was then followed by soon-to-be dads going through some purification rites. Records which were gathered also show that such purification rites usually involve physical mutilation and intense pain.

The couvade rituals have been identified and reported in very diverse people in various locations around the world – Basques of Spain, Chinese, Africans, Papua of New Guinea, France, American Indians and several others. Interestingly, the researchers noticed that in almost all the observed cases, the role of the mother is often minimized just to maximize the roles of the father. Some contemporary examples of the couvade ritual include British Guiana where an expectant dad has to avoid consuming animal foods before his partner delivers their baby. As soon as his partner delivers, then he may only eat cassava meal. Also, there is the Ainus of northern Japan as well as the Witotos of South America where a soon-to-be dad stays in bed and continues to display his wife's labor pains until the new-born is brought to him and then his wife and friends will summarily feed and pamper him. There are places where ritualistic couvade is still present to some extent, especially in industrialized societies; for instance, in England, many people are of the view that the pains of childbirth experienced by a woman is relieved proportionately by the sufferings of her male partner.

Why Couvade Ritual?

To some extent, the reasons why couvade rituals exist isn't very clear. Many anthropologists have disclosed that different people have provided various reasons, but they have also been able to identify some common beliefs behind the ritual. The first of reasons or beliefs behind the couvade ritual is that when expectant fathers mimic their pregnant partners, they protect the vulnerable mother and infant from evil spirits by simply attracting them to himself. Another reason is that such rituals help to spiritually strengthen the bond that exists between the father and child. Some believe that a father possesses a stronger or higher supernatural presence than his female partner, which explains why he is needed to guide the new-born into the world. Some people also believe that the primary reason for the ritual is to enable the father to socially assert his paternity. Generally, the majority of anthropologists infer that the purpose of the ritual is to offer soon-to-be dads the opportunity to become more involved with the pregnancy than the simple sexual activity that took place about ten months earlier.

One of the striking things about the couvade ritual is that similar forms of the ritual have been performed in different tribes and people around the world with diverse cultures which doesn't even have any historical links between them. So, what does this imply? Some anthropologists believe that the ritual is not a mere cultural practice; instead, it has a fundamental and universal underpinning to it.

Presently, there are debates on whether or not couvade ritual is adaptive. However, the truth is that it still represents an opportunity for soon-to-be dads to become more involved with their pregnant partner in a socially acceptable way. This may, in turn, lead to increased viability of the children.

So, what's the relationship between couvade ritual and couvade syndrome? *Some researchers believe that couvade syndrome is now an updated version of couvade ritual with newly introduced differences.* Unlike couvade ritual, where expectant men observe certain rules and cultures while mimicking their pregnant partner, couvade syndrome involves the "real" thing; men experience real symptom or symptoms that are associated with couvade. Well, this doesn't imply that the men who observe couvade ritual were only mimicking their symptoms; they may actually suffer from both – mimicking and actual manifestations of couvade. Another aspect that's interesting to note also is the fact that ritualistic couvade tends to place more emphasis on the relationship between a father and his offspring, but on the other hand, couvade syndrome is often linked to an expectant dad's sympathy for his partner. I must not fail to mention here too that some investigators strongly believe that ritualistic couvade and couvade syndrome all serve similar functions – representing the responses of developmental crisis.

What causes Couvade syndrome?

If you're an expectant father who is experiencing some symptoms of pregnancy, then you may find it a bit strange at first. In our society, people and health professionals are usually interested in pregnant women. They often encourage them to talk about possible symptoms they are experiencing as well as the common ones she may not be experiencing as well. What about the home of a pregnant woman? If your wife is pregnant, for example, then some of the commonest topics you may discuss with your wife and family are things related to her frustrated incapacitations due to her symptoms. Well, there is also the immense joy of expecting the newest member of your family. This explains the reason why a good number of mental health professionals have examined a wide range of hypothesis ranging from the guilt of having been the cause of the transformation in a partner's body to jealousy about the inability of a man to carry a child and in some cases, it has also been attributed to selfish attention-seeking. But there are some of the obvious sources of at least a symptom of the syndrome. This has to do with the issue of weight for a husband. It's thought that a pregnant wife usually does more cooking and shopping due to her cravings, and there is also an increased consumption of food which she requires while pregnant. This is also believed by some health professionals to be the cause of other symptoms like indigestion and heartburn.

One of the available explanations for the couvade syndrome is that it's a psychiatric disorder which is more common among Europeans than Americans. Experts who believe in this explanation attribute the symptoms to jealousy – the man being jealous of his wife's ability to become pregnant and give birth. For others also who believe in this explanation, they think that the syndrome could either be caused by male guilt of getting a woman pregnant or sibling rivalry – a situation where a husband sees his wife as a competitor that he needs to outperform. We shall be looking at various theories about couvade in the next chapter. Another group of Canadian researchers believe that it is caused by biological changes which take place in the body of expectant fathers. According to the researchers, the sample of blood and saliva they obtained from expectant fathers revealed higher levels of estradiol (this is a female hormone) than that of a control group of men who weren't expecting a child. I must point out here that the researchers have actually disclosed that there is a need to check their findings by studying different groups of men from different cultures around the world. Some believe that couvade syndrome is as a result of a changed social role. So, in this case, expectant men experience this syndrome as a way to "work through" their feelings of taking up the responsibilities and social expectations that are associated with fatherhood.

Another possible cause of the syndrome is the expectant father's attachment or closeness to the fetus. Some men who are prone to experience several symptoms of couvade syndrome have deep empathy for their pregnant partner and strong attachments to their child. For instance, according to a seminal study which took place in 1983, a sample of first-time expectant fathers (specifically white middle-class) revealed a remarkable correlation between an increased closeness of a father to the fetus (which involved confirmation via the wife's pregnancy symptoms, hearing and feeling the kicking of the unborn child) with the occurrence of about six different physical manifestations of couvade syndrome. According to the investigators, they believe that the symptoms expectant men experience where actually a reflection of how attached they are to their unborn child as well as how involved they are during the pregnancy period. We will discuss more about the possible reasons why men experience couvade symptoms when we look into various theories in this field.

Symptoms of Couvade Syndrome

Undoubtedly, most fathers are familiar with some of the symptoms of pregnancy that women experience. But soon-to-be fathers with couvade syndrome also experience certain symptoms that are similar to their pregnant wives. Are you a father who's expecting a baby soon? Do you find yourself also battling to satisfy your cravings just like your pregnant wife whose case is understandable? Well, if you're thinking that all you're doing is sharing the snacks with your pregnant partner, it may not be entirely true. Have you ever considered the possibility of sharing the symptoms with your partner? If you've experienced specific changes in your life or done something that made you ask, "Wait a minute, who's pregnant here?" It's most likely you're having what some men experience – the couvade syndrome.

Many international studies have over the last decade attempted to learn more about the frequency, time course, as well as the type of couvade syndrome symptoms. Some of the symptoms they have investigated include psychological and/or physical symptoms, the patterns of such symptoms and the duration and withdrawal over pregnancy. For instance, Trethowan and Conlin in the UK sought to identify the frequency, duration and incidence of the symptoms all through the duration of a normal pregnancy (nine months) in 327 men whose age was averagely 29 years and they all had pregnant partners. They compared this group of men to another group of 221 married men with an average age of 35 years and whose partners weren't pregnant. The study discovered that a total of 186 soon-to-be fathers (representing 57 percent) showed over two symptoms of couvade syndrome during gestation which lasted for nine months as opposed to 101 (representing 46 percent) in the second group. Among the most frequent symptoms the men experienced include nausea, anxiety, toothache, loss of appetite and sickness.

They experienced the peak of the symptoms in the third month of pregnancy, but this seemed to diminish in the second trimester. They also noticed a rise in the symptoms again during the nine months. One other factor the investigators need to consider (which they also acknowledged) is the age difference. I must also state here that there was no evidence to prove the reliability as well as the validity of the study instrument.

One straightforward way to explain the symptoms that have been identified is to divide them into different groups, but I'll briefly talk about some of the commonest ones. The first group is the *"gastrointestinal"* symptoms of couvade which includes:

- Abdominal pain
- Vomiting
- Heartburn
- Abdominal bloating
- Nausea

Another group of symptoms has to do with different kinds of pains and aches, such as:

- Backaches
- Leg Cramps

- Stomach aches
- Toothaches
- Urogenital irritations

The third group of symptoms of couvade syndrome are behavioral manifestations which include:

- Changes in appetite (it could be an increase or decrease in appetite)
- Unintentional weight gain
- Restlessness
- Libido reduction
- Changes in sleep habits
- Increased anxiety

Based on the results of reports from studies, the group of symptoms that are most commonly reported by soon-to-be dads are the ones that are significantly gastrointestinal such as abdominal pain, nausea and cramping. Let's look at some of these symptoms in detail.

Nausea

One of the most prevalent symptoms of pregnancy is morning sickness, but it's not exclusive to expectant mothers or only mornings. Generally, this infamous pregnancy challenge is often associated with an uptick in the hormones of a pregnant woman during pregnancy. Interestingly, some soon-to-be fathers find themselves running to the toilet. The issue of morning sickness for men may be attributed to anxiety and possible changes in diet, especially for men who try to relieve stress through eating.

Changes in Sexual Urge

The sex drive of a woman during pregnancy can either go up (good news for you) or remain neutral. It can also do both in one week. For some expectant mums, there is a surge in their sexual drive, especially during the second trimester. But this isn't always the case because some women may even be self-conscious of their bodies, uncomfortable or may even be too tired to show interest in it.

For soon-to-be fathers, their sexual appetite is highly unpredictable. While some men may be overwhelmed by the transformation, which always reminds them of the increased responsibilities they will soon have to deal with. Some parents may choose to stay away from sex entirely because they may be scared of hurting their baby. Some expectant fathers are energized by the fact that they are going to have a baby, while the mere thought of a new baby may lead to exhaustion for others.

Did you find the category you belong? Regardless of what your sex appetite looks like while your wife is pregnant, always remember to remain intimate. Sex happens to be one out of several ways to be intimate with your partner, and I will be sharing with you several tips to help you boost your sex drive while dealing with couvade symptoms.

Anxiety

Another common symptom of the syndrome is anxiety. Even the calmest expectant fathers may also witness heartburn, restless nights as well as bouts of fatigue. What could be the possible cause of anxiety? The truth is that male and female partners are often confronted with multiple concerns and anxiety, courtesy of pregnancy. According to experts, this could be as a result of the impact of the changing dyadic relationship to a triadic one. Of course, there is also the anxiety that fathers experience due to the transition as well as preparation for fatherhood.

Other concerns include the health of the woman during gestation and childbirth as well as that of the unborn child. Several studies have focused their work on the relationship between the couvade syndrome and anxiety. Some studies revealed that expectant fathers with the syndrome usually report more anxiety. In some cases, the anxiety actually increased when their pregnant wives were anxious regarding their pregnancy and the eventual delivery of their child. This perhaps explains why the researcher concluded that the anxiety experienced by women appears to be a crucial factor in the development of the syndrome than the one experienced by the expectant father. Is your wife always anxious about the state of health of her baby or how the delivery will turn out? If yes, then this could also be a reason why you're having one of the symptoms of the syndrome – simply a transference of, or shared anxiety between you and your wife.

Mood Swings

Of course, it's common for your pregnant partner to switch from sadness to joy, sweetness to (extreme) crankiness, and from tranquility to anxiety. But you may also experience the same kind of mood swings. Although hormones often intensify mood swings, men and women still have the same underlying cause – nerves. As an expectant father, you must have realized by now that having a baby is indeed a big deal, especially in the middle of the night. I'm sure your life would never be the same once your child is born. In fact, chances are that it's already changing right now, and this could result in more mixed emotions and less sleep. It's actually natural to experience such worrying, but you should understand that as a new dad, you need a lot of practice to enable you to balance out the highs and lows of being a new father. Remember, there is no perfect dad and you're not likely to be the first one here. You just have to relax and realize that the best time to practice is now before your baby arrives.

Aches and Pains

A look at some of the symptoms of sympathetic pregnancy that we've talked about before shows that most of them have possible causes. Well, some are also mysterious and this is one of them. Are you in any way experiencing certain body pains such as headaches, toothaches, leg cramps and backaches? These are some of the pains that men in different studies on couvade syndrome complain of, so you're not alone. In fact, some men also disclosed that they sometimes have pains in the same spot just at the same time their partners are experiencing it. This is one group of symptoms which researchers have not been able to understand or give any physical explanations as to the causes. However, several studies have revealed that some men reported symptoms such as changes in their sleeping patterns, restlessness, reduced libido, backache as well as urogenital irritations.

Weight Gain

For a mummy-to-be, a bigger belly may be a given, but what may appear strange is when a man gains over 14 pounds while his partner is pregnant. Well, several factors have been suggested to cause this increase in weight for expectant fathers. Perhaps one of the best ways to look at the cause of weight gain in soon-to-be fathers is to look at the study of a US team of researchers. They studied the parental weight pattern, which is popular among marmosets as well as cotton-top tamarins from the time of conception to birth. The team weighed 33 pregnant mums and 25 prospective dads every month, and during this period, the food supply for the animals wasn't altered. Also, their food wasn't increased during the gestation periods for the tamarins (six months) and marmosets (five months). The result of their observation shows that the weight of the males increased by an average of 10 percent during the pregnancy.

According to Toni Zeigler (leader of the research at the University of Wisconsin-Madison National Primate Research Centre), most of the females gained weight during the final weeks of gestation. They attributed the weight gain of the males to increased production of prolactin – this is also the same hormone that encourages the production of milk in females.

According to the study, there was an increased level of prolactin in males halfway through pregnancy during the period when females witness a spike in the levels of corticosterone. In case you're a bit confused about the word corticosterone; it's a hormone that's involved in sending and receiving pheromones (we'll look at pheromones in chapter two). According to Zeigler, studies in birds show that prolactin actually promotes paternal care since an increased level of the hormone in birds cause the fathers to feed the chicks frequently, but it's unclear what other roles prolactin play in primates or humans. He further disclosed that since tamarind males make excellent fathers, and even remain with one partner for life, it could help explain some of the biological changes that are essential in humans to produce good fathers.

But what are other possible reasons why soon-to-be dads could be experiencing weight gain? Well, cortisol is another possible reason. Commonly known as the *"stress hormone,"* the volume of cortisol secreted during moments of anxiety is usually higher than the normal levels. Since the stress hormone helps to regulate insulin as well as blood sugar levels, it's possible that as an expectant dad, your body may think it's hungry when it's really not. Another reason why some men may experience an increase in the size of their belly is that cortisol decides where the extra pounds are located in the body, which is often the belly.

Chapter II

Latest Research on Couvade Syndrome

As earlier mentioned, men also are affected by pregnancy just like their partners in several ways that have to do with their psychological and physiological constitution. A good number of researchers have attempted to learn more about the syndrome. In 2007, Dr. Brennan and his associates embarked on a review of the literature on various psycho-physiological symptoms (of couvade syndrome) that soon-to-be dads experience during the gestation period of their partners. In a bid to obtain both archival and contemporary information required for the study, the search covered the period starting from 1950-2006. Their findings discovered that the global incidence of sympathetic pregnancy varies significantly as shown by various studies. In the UK, for instance, the couvade syndrome is quite unknown; however, there are estimates of reported cases which ranges from 11 to 50 percent. They also observed that the level of couvade syndrome in Sweden is 20 percent and a varied incidence of 25 to 50 percent was reported for the USA. Undoubtedly, the facts about the occurrence of the syndrome in other locations around the world is proof of the extent of variability of the syndrome. This is evident with the incidence in Thailand, which is 61 percent while China has 68 percent of cases of sympathy pregnancy. Interestingly, in Australia, the syndrome is rarely reported by soon-to-be dads, and several factors could actually cause this. For instance, it could be a reflection of how reluctant soon-to-be dads are in reporting such cases. It could also be an issue with diagnostic accuracy or a total lack of interest in this phenomenon by healthcare professionals. The global variability (ranging from 11-97 percent), which is evident in the data obtained by Dr Brennan and his team is caused by various factors. For instance, disclosing such symptoms experienced by men may be seen as an anathema, especially in what most people see as a "macho" culture. Also, some men may end up concealing the physical symptoms they may be experiencing simply because they are ashamed to admit it since it could mean weakness on their part. The aftermath of the study revealed that sympathetic pregnancy is undoubtedly a global phenomenon which men in different countries around the world experience.

The study concluded that the symptoms of couvade syndrome are clearly linked to pregnancy, and most of these symptoms often disappear during the postpartum period. However, there is a need for further studies that make use of a qualitative approach which permits expectant fathers to talk about their experiences of the sympathetic pregnancy in their language. Also, such studies should use a quantitative approach that's based on the themes as well as sub-themes developed from the quantitative study as this would help to estimate how severe the manifestations are and also its impact on the level of distress for men as well as their partners.

When it comes to the role anxiety plays in couvade syndrome, the study observed that some expectant fathers reported more anxiety and the anxiety was more common when their partner was also more anxious about the impending birth. Also, some studies confirmed that the level of pregnancy-related symptoms which soon-to-be fathers experienced was directly related to their level of anxiety. Well, Dr Brennan and his associated pointed out that one challenge with some studies in the aspect of anxiety and stress is the fact that they often used stress and anxiety interchangeably instead of treating them separately when determining their relationship with the symptoms of sympathetic pregnancy and obtaining better definitions for each issue.

Expectant Father's Involvement and Couvade Syndrome

Some studies have also examined the relationship between the extent of involvement of expectant men, role preparation and sympathetic pregnancy. Interestingly, most of the studies were able to demonstrate that indeed, the higher the level of participation of male partners as well as a greater level of role preparation displayed, the more they show couvade symptoms. This implies that symptoms of couvade syndrome are likely going to increase when men tend to be more prepared and involved in handling several roles while helping their pregnant partners. In fact, one study went further to discover that the seriousness, number, as well as the duration of symptoms of couvade syndrome experienced by soon-to-be dads was positively correlated to the effective involvements of soon-to-be dads when compared to non-expectant dads. The expectant fathers' involvement here relates to their attachment to the unborn child. However, it's crucial to state here that some studies that attempted to explore this the correlation between the level of involvement and number of symptoms provided contradictory results.

The Biology of Dads

Dr Arthur Brennan of Kingston University and St. George's University of London is among the researchers who have made efforts to establish the fact that soon-to-be fathers experience several pregnancy symptoms earlier shared in this chapter such as labor pains, swollen stomach (baby bumps) or nausea. His focus was to confirm whether these symptoms experienced by expectant fathers are the result of the type of hormonal changes that their pregnant partners experienced.

Dr. Brennan was of the view that the cause of couvade syndrome may be an increase in the level of the hormone "prolactin" which is common in breastfeeding mothers. The presence of prolactin in men leads to a reduction in the levels of testosterone which in turn ends up bringing out the "softer" as well as emotional side of men. This, in his view, may be the reason for the way expectant fathers behave, like those who cry when their child is born. In the words of Dr. Brennan;

"It seems fathers may be just as much a victim of their hormones as their pregnant partners."

One of the experiments conducted by Dr Brenan was the one which featured in the BBC 4 program, *"The Biology of Dads."* In the experiment, the prolactin levels of Michel Gauvin, who was a new father, was monitored shortly after his daughter Matilde was born. While cradling his daughter, the level of his prolactin increased by 20 percent within 15 minutes. Interestingly, Michel had earlier witnessed several symptoms of sympathetic pregnancy such as weight gain, increased cravings for stodgy food and nausea while his wife was pregnant. Dr. Brennan disclosed that expectant fathers who experience several pregnancy symptoms might actually be going through normal hormonal changes which enables them to be well prepared for their responsibilities as fathers. He was interested in finding out whether there is a physiological basis for the symptoms of soon-to-be dads even though such symptoms are mainly seen as a psychosomatic disorder.

Theories of Couvade Syndrome

It's crucial for us to take a more in-depth look at efforts made by researchers to explain the factors that cause sympathetic pregnancy. In a bid to identify the origins of the couvade syndrome, several theories have actually been put forward and we shall be starting with psychosocial theories.

Psychosocial Theories

This theory has to do with the marginalization of men during the pregnancy of their partners and the birth of their child. One of the theories that fall under this category which is the *"parturition envy and resurgence of childhood conflicts"* suggest that sympathetic pregnancy is as a result of the father's envy of his partner's procreative ability. A psychoanalytical theorist, Bohem who was actually the first to coin the term *"parturition envy"* is of the view that soon-to-be fathers see parturition and conception as something quite complicated and uncanny. This is because such processes appear very mysterious to them and as such, they desire to partake of the processes or end up in intense envy for those who have the capacity – women. Other experts also believe that the psychosomatic symptoms experienced by expectant fathers during gestation may be an indication of their unconscious desire to also have a taste of the partner's pregnancy themselves. So, if you're experiencing some symptoms of couvade syndrome, then this may be the reason why you're experiencing it. For other researchers in this field, sympathetic pregnancy serves as some kind of catalyst for the occurrence of ambivalence as well as the resurgence of *"oedipal conflicts."* I guess you may be confused by the term oedipal conflicts. It refers to the unconscious emotions of a child (especially male children) which usually involves the desire to sexually possess the parent of opposite sex and at the same time exclude the other parent of the same sex.

One of such theories is men's marginalization during pregnancy and delivery. The focus of psychoanalytical theories is on the inner conflicts of men, but the focus of psychosocial theories is not on the internal conflicts of expectant fathers, but on their role and status in the course of the pregnancy. They suggest that such roles have an impact on the prospective dad's health. So, men's marginalization during their partner's gestation and deliver is seen as a crucial antecedent of the syndrome. Although the role of motherhood may make up a vital defining attribute for every woman, this may not be the same for fatherhood and men. The *"maternity careers"* of expectant women have been endorsed medically, socially and commercially in contrast to expecting fathers. According to a famous anthropologist, Margaret Mead, the issue of civilization was satisfactorily and adequately defining the role of men to give them that sense of achievement that women get naturally when they give birth to a child. But the kind of recognition accorded to most men by society is playing a peripheral role during pregnancy as well as childbirth, and they may just accept such recognition as a mere token acknowledgement that they exist.

There is also the kind of relationship that exists between men and women with their unborn child, which is also different. While the awareness of as well as the maternal relationship with the unborn child of a woman takes place via internalized, tactile, kinesthetic and sensory experience, it's entirely different for the man. A soon-to-be dad usually experiences his unborn child vicariously, and his pregnant partner controls access to the child. Consequently, men may end up developing what some experts called *"pseudo-pregnancy"* along with its somatic symptoms. Well, the truth is that not everyone will accept the idea that expectant men are being given less recognition in a matricentric world. For instance, the feminist perspective actually rejects the notion of male marginalization proposed by some experts which we earlier discussed. They actually argue for the progressive increase in the number of men's gender roles which involves an increase in their participation in several domestic chores as well as a more child-centered approach to family life. Consequently, more men are now becoming very active in the pregnancy and birth process, which was once seen as primarily an exclusive heritage for women. It's also important to note that some men actually attempt to maintain separation in a bid to uphold the paternal roles and traditional male values.

Fatherhood as a Developmental Crisis

Another psychosocial theory is men's transition to fatherhood as a season of developmental crisis. The transition to parenthood for women is often associated with several psychosocial changes and this transition for men may actually equate to that of motherhood. This is the position of this theory. The truth is that although both parents share the pregnancy experience, the kind of emotions and concerns it induces differs between each gender. For some experts who believe in this theory, they propose that impending fatherhood remains one of the most crucial periods in human life.

Men accept the pregnancy of their partners without physical changes that will reinforce the reality of such pregnancy. In cases like that, some prospective fathers may experience physical symptoms that tend to be higher than the average levels during their partner's pregnancy. So, this implies that couvade occurs in response to the developmental crisis of pregnancy. Men are believed to be *"laboring for relevance"* in their struggle as new fathers. The struggle of prospective fathers has to do with adding their paternal role to their identity. In the course of their transition to fatherhood, soon-to-be fathers need to accept their changed sense of self. But experts say that this developmental process is in some cases, incomplete which implies that all men don't end up achieving actualization as involved dads.

Identification with the Pregnant Partner

According to some studies, one of the possible explanations for couvade syndrome, which is also one of the simplest ones is that the symptoms of sympathetic pregnancy are a somatic expression of anxiety. Also, some experts in this field are of the view that soon-to-be fathers express somatic symptoms because of their high level of identification with their pregnant partner. So, the purpose of this attempt at identification is to resolve possible ambivalence that men feel towards their partners.

Talking about ambivalence about fatherhood, couvade symptoms are also regarded as the somatic expression of soon-to-be dad's ambivalence toward his dad and then himself as a father. In one particular case of a psychotic father who expressed his anger over the relationship with his dad; he was actually ambivalent about being a dad because he believed he had a poor role model. Consequently, he expressed his psychosis in the delusion that he wasn't the father of the unborn child. This undoubtedly is a representation of the inner conflict he was having.

Fetus as Rival

Another psychoanalytical theory is known as *"fetus as rival."* this theory proposes that soon-to-be dads may perceive their unborn child as someone who's trying to deprive them of maternal attention. So, in this case, the primary concern for expectant fathers is that they may finally lose their partner to their child when finally born. Researchers in this field such as May, have actually identified that there is indeed an increasing distance between some prospective fathers and their pregnant wives, especially in the first trimester. They, therefore, concluded that this rift (especially among fathers whose dependency needs weren't sufficiently satisfied as children) must have been as a result of excessive jealousy of the unborn child. So, could it be that you may be having the couvade syndrome simply because you're unconsciously jealous of your unborn child? Well, that may be the case for some people. In fact, some experts in this field further argued that for men who even married mainly to satisfy their dependency needs, they might end up unconsciously seeing the fetus as a rival for dependency. Well, it doesn't end there as the pregnancy may also open the eyes of such dads to the truth that they are no longer children but adults who have increased responsibilities as fathers. This ends up frustrating a prospective father's dependency needs.

Another aspect that I believe we need to look at is the issue of sibling rivalry; when an expectant father sees the unborn child as a competitor, then it may eventually reactivate earlier conflicts of childhood – sibling rivalry. This kind of response may be common among men who had younger siblings and ended up losing maternal care and attention as a result of the emergence of their younger siblings. A number of psychoanalysts describe this as some kind of symbolic re-interpretation of the unborn child as the historical sibling while the pregnant woman is now seen as the biological mother whose attention they failed to get. Well, there have been several criticisms of the psychoanalytical theories; for instance, a good number of psychoanalytic theories have not been scientifically tested. Also, their alleged causes of the couvade syndrome (the subconscious interpretations and conflicts) were primarily obtained from reports and case studies which are prone to subjective interpretations. So, it's hard to generalize.

Paternal Transition Theory

Undoubtedly, pregnancy is sometimes stressful for both parents of a child, especially when it's a first child. This is the focus of the paternal transition theory. This theory is of the view that the process of becoming a father is quite stressful, which involves changes that the body must have to respond to biologically to enable it make sense of it. This theory, just like the two theories, also takes a look at the emotional conflicts that prospective men face. But it tends to differ from psychoanalytical theories by suggesting that what gives rise to couvade syndrome is man's closeness to the unborn child (the fetus).

Several studies have explored the relationship between men's role preparation, involvement in pregnancy and couvade syndrome. Interestingly, most of the studies have successfully demonstrated that there is an increase in the frequency of the display of couvade symptoms with a higher level of men's involvement as well as a greater level of role preparation in men. In fact, one study clearly identified that there was a strong and positive correlation between active involvement during pregnancy and the duration, seriousness and number of symptoms displayed by soon-to-be dads in comparison to men who were not expecting a baby.

Paternity Issues

Some experts also suggest that paternity issues are among the causes of couvade. The idea here is that couvade is just a mechanism that gives a father an opportunity to repudiate possible doubts that exists about being the true father of the child after birth. In fact, some believe that couvade is useful in establishing spiritual paternity. They noted that it's of significant biological value for a father and mother to comprise the human family. So, if the existence of certain traditional customs as well as rules are meant to foster a social situation where a father is brought close to his child, and if such traditions such as couvade rituals help to draw a father's attention to his offspring, then couvade is indeed beneficial. It implies that it helps to provide the essential stimulus and expression for paternal tendencies. In summary, experts who believe in the paternity crisis conclude that the aim of couvade is to accentuate the principle of legitimacy – the fulfilment of a child's need for a father.

Sexuality and Gender Identity Issues

For some men, the duration of their partner's pregnancy is a time of overwhelming changes. Some researchers actually reported that for some soon-to-be dads, the panic that's aroused during the period might manifest itself in transient homosexuality and temporary impotence. Remember, one of the common symptoms of couvade that has been reported were cases of a reduction in libido. They believe that latent homosexuality may become activated in some soon-to-be dads with an increased expression of homosexual impulses and a decrease in the desire for heterosexual behavior in the course of the pregnancy. For some men, couvade symptoms may be seen as involuntary manifestations of underlying female gender identity in some men. Based on the works of Monroe and Monroe; they carried out a study of males in three different societies and discovered that soon-to-be dads having somatic symptoms also exhibited feminine responses on overt measures of gender identity.

Couvade Syndrome and Evolution

The notion of evolutionary fitness and natural selection has also formed the basis for all biological explanations regarding the function of behavior. For instance, all practices that aid in increasing the success of reproduction are seen as "fit." In the field of evolution, two contradictory behaviors are commonly practiced by male animals. They are infanticide (the killing of their offspring) and paternal care – two phenomena often witnessed in males of the same species. The two behaviors have proved over time to be adaptive behaviors that are maintained by natural selection. In carnivores, infanticide is quite common as seen in primates, lions, rodents and several other species.

There are several benefits that male killers enjoy. The first one has to do with the fact that male killers may kill infants for food. Another reason for killing infants is that when a male kills an infant, then it increases the possibility that the female (mother of the slain infant) may cease lactation and this increases the chances of mating with the new male. The third reason for infanticide is that some males do it in a bid to avoid taking care of the infants, especially the ones that are not biologically related to them.

Undoubtedly, we all see cases of infanticide on TV, so it's still a common trend among mammals. But males can't advance their genetic line when they engage in the indiscriminate killing of infants. This is because their own could also be among the infants that will eventually be killed. But when you take a look at some of the animals earlier mentioned, you will also discover that some of them alter their behavior – from killing infants to non-infanticidal. In fact, in some cases, we've seen instances where such mammals that were prone to infanticide, take care of young ones, especially when they are expecting their offspring. This shift in behavior is not also directed only at their offspring when they eventually recognize it, but to all young. This kind of change usually takes place while their female partner is pregnant, so the males are actually drawn into a "paternal state" shortly before the birth of their offspring.

Experts believe that males who previously kill infants are brought into a "paternal state" in a bid to ensure that they don't hurt or kill their young, so they cease from harming all young they see whether they are related or not. But how does this relate to couvade syndrome and even humans? Well, cases of infanticide in humans are extremely rare; however, the information from animals can also help us understand the biological explanation for couvade syndrome in humans which could be likened to the cessation of infanticide in mammals. Some experts suggest that it's most unlikely that humans were unique without similar changes that occur in other mammals as explained. Several changes in behavior that have been identified in soon-to-be dads before the birth of their child are quite surprising. It's believed that this trait proves to be genetically fit, considering the fact that human offspring need a significant level of parental effort.

According to a definition of what parental in men means, *"it has to do with awareness, perceptions, thoughts, sensations and feelings pertaining to the involvement of expectant dads with their kids."* Several studies have identified that fathers having a high level of attachment scores were also associated with partners who had low personal involvement with their children. So, this tends to confirm the fact that such fathers with high attachment to their children may instinctively be "filling the gap" which was created by the partner with a low attachment to their children. Based on this perspective, it's therefore possible that couvade syndrome is crucial to ensure successful childrearing and this will further increase the genetic fitness of the father.

Hormonal Changes in Soon-to-be Dads

Although we've earlier talked about the impact of hormonal changes on the level of couvade symptoms in expectant dads, it's important to take a more in-depth look at it. Researchers have identified evidence to suggest that some of the shifts noticed in the behavior of expectant fathers were caused by physiological changes that are in several ways similar to the ones in pregnant females that induce the onset of maternal care. Based on the results of various studies in rodents and nonhuman primates, there is evidence to suggest that in serum concentrations, a decrease of testosterone and increase of prolactin are linked with the expression of paternal behavior. Well, there hasn't been any study to prove that a functional relationship truly exists between the hormonal changes and paternal behavior; some studies have suggested that this could be possible. Some human studies about the paternal hormonal changes in new and soon-to-be dads have provided some promising results to support the possibility of hormonal changes as a cause of couvade syndrome. For instance, an article that was published in 2000 by Storey and his associates revealed that hormonal changes which take place in humans are partly responsible for preparing expectant fathers to care for their new-born properly. The focus of the study was to show that human hormonal changes play a significant role in preparing soon-to-be dads to care for their offspring. The researchers studied the changes that occur in four hormones: estradiol, cortisol, prolactin and testosterone.

The result of their study disclosed that expectant dads witnessed a remarkable pre and postnatal changes in every single hormone measured and the patterns of change noticed paralleling the types found in women. Although they noticed hormonal correlations between partners, they didn't find possible behavioral, physiological and environmental cues that could be the cause. A further review of the study also shows that men who have lower levels of testosterone were more responsive to infant cues and this further supports the idea that there is a link between lower testosterone and greater paternal responsiveness. In summary, their findings suggest that the decrease in the level of testosterone from a control group to the prenatal period and the early postnatal period may actually foster paternal responsiveness by lowering the tendencies of men to engage in behaviors that are non-nurturing.

Another hormone that was studied is estradiol, and it was observed that estradiol levels reached its peak in soon-to-be dads in the late prenatal period. While there are reports to suggest that estradiol is crucial for enhancing mammalian maternal behavior, the researchers could only identify a little evidence to prove that there is a relationship between the levels of estradiol and paternal responsiveness in humans. This was however linked to a sampling error, but it could also imply that there is no relationship at all.

The third hormone is prolactin and during the study, the level of prolactin peaked both in expectant dads and women in the late prenatal period and even high in the early prenatal period. There was also a noticeable increase in the level of prolactin in men who displayed greater responsiveness to the cry of a baby as well as in men who reported having more symptoms of couvade syndrome. Although the level of prolactin in men was quite lower than that of women, stage-specific changes actually correlated between partners. The outcome of the results supports the suggestion that the decreasing testosterone and increasing prolactin are adaptive in humans – a biparental species. Finally, there was an increase in the cortisol level both in men and women immediately before the birth of a baby and also a decrease in the level during the postnatal period. In addition, during labor, both partners among the couples sampled in the research recorded a 75 percent increase in the level of cortisol. The researchers observed a positive relationship between cortisol levels and the responsiveness of behaviors towards new-borns.

Considering the results of animal studies, experts are of the view that the identified patterns of increase in the cortisol level in men suggest that the rise in the level of cortisol during the late stage of pregnancy as well as during labor may assist fathers to concentrate and become more attached to their infants. The results of some studies have also revealed that the lower level of testosterone in modern fathers often leads to less risk-taking in them. In fact, it further fosters better child-rearing ability in expectant dads and this is believed to have evolved in men over five to six million years ago. Also, it's been observed that soon-to-be dads with lowered testosterone were actually more successful in raising new-borns, and their genes were even passed along.

This position was further supported by a US research which discovered that the levels of testosterone in expectant dads dropped by as much as 34 percent after their partners gave birth. The researchers believed that since testosterone is the hormone that's associated with aggressive and dominant behavior, then men, just like women are also wired for parenthood. The researchers believe that this change where men become softer and more caring after the birth of their child implies that men have evolved to protect their kids as well as their genes.

According to Dr Pacey, the reduction in the level of testosterone does not actually make fathers more child-friendly; instead, it helps to change their priorities so that they can invest more in their new-born. A similar phenomenon occurred when another group of US scientists studied male marmosets (which is among the few primates apart from humans where both genders take care of their offspring). As soon as the researchers gave the male marmosets a whiff of their babies' scent, there was a significant drop in their level of testosterone within 20 minutes. Unfortunately, several factors could be responsible for the drop in testosterone and this could be the as a result of an increased level of cortisol which lowers testosterone production when it rises. So, some experts argue that the rise in testosterone levels could be in response to stress, especially during the pregnancy period of their partner. This makes it unclear whether the drop in testosterone is specific to evolution.

The Possible Influence of Pheromones on Couvade Syndrome

One of the areas that has attracted much interest both from the scientific communities and the public is the existence of human pheromones. This has undoubtedly led to a spike in the number of researchers working in the area of human physiology. So, what are pheromones?

"They are regarded as airborne chemical signals that a person releases into the environment, which in turn affects the behavior or physiology of other members of the same species."
Here are some facts you should know about pheromones:

- They are just like hormones, but unlike hormones which work within the body, pheromones work outside the body.
- We have about four different types of pheromones – signaler, modulator, releaser and primer.
- Generally, pheromones induce activity in other individuals and this includes sexual arousal.
- Although several studies have examined some chemicals to determine whether they have pheromone action in humans, the evidence obtained so far is still weak.
- One of the ways insects communicate is with pheromones

It has been observed to be secreted from the apocrine sweat glands primarily discovered in the axilla as well as other parts of the skin (in a lesser extent) such as the labia majora, mammary areola and the cacuminal region. In humans, pheromones are known to excite certain regions of our brain (and also an organ known as the vomeronasal organ) to affect social behavior, regulate ovulation and several others. Actually, the findings in this field are sufficient to prove that humans can and do produce pheromones.

Now we've seen some of the theories concerning the etiology of couvade syndrome and this is a confirmation that it is indeed a well-documented and widespread trend. However, the explanation of the phenomenon is still not well established. There are several psychoanalytical theories concerning the causes of couvade, but most of these theories are inconclusive. Majority of these reports also lack empirical data and are significantly incongruous. But almost all psychosocial investigators have agreed that sympathetic pregnancy may be an indication of ineffective coping and request for assistance in managing crisis. The reason why I shared some of these theories is to enlighten you on the fact that the phenomenon has been in existence. Interestingly, if you're having several symptoms of couvade, then you're not alone; in fact, many expectant fathers may also be experiencing it and some may be aware but choose to conceal it while others may not understand the reason why they are experiencing certain changes in their lives.

50

Chapter III

Ways to Fight Symptoms of Couvade Syndrome

When it comes to the treatment of couvade syndrome, presently no standard mainstream treatment has been recommended for treating the symptoms. This is because couvade syndrome isn't usually mentioned in medical books. Some studies have indicated that soon-to-be dads with symptoms of couvade actually take more medication. Well, those who take medicine for symptoms such as aches and gastrointestinal symptoms may likely do so mainly to control the symptoms and not to treat sympathetic pregnancy itself.

While there may not be any known medication, there are several things you can do to effectively manage the symptoms and even get significant relief from couvade syndrome. It's important to note also that most couvade symptoms often leave as soon as the baby is born while some men have reported that their symptoms also disappeared before birth. This chapter will focus on some of the things you can do to fight these symptoms.

Fighting against the Common Fear of Becoming a Father

Interestingly, those who may appear as extra prepared to become a dad may sometimes discover that they're a little freaked out as well. Even when they are having their third or fifth child, a good number of men still experience most of the fears they still had when they had their first child. Well, those having their first child are definitely not spared from the fear that most men have when they're going to have a baby. The fear that arises in the hearts of many soon-to-be dads can be quite frightening and, in some cases, it could be paralyzing. Well, you don't have to give such fears the power to keep you worried or even allow them to influence your decisions. In fact, some men suggest that the fear of having a baby has prevented them from even having children. They have accepted the myths about fatherhood which the society told them or the ones they harbor in their minds. If you're in this category or if you're battling the fears of fatherhood shortly after your partner broke the news to you, then remember that it's just fear. The voice of fear you hear from the society or within you is the same voice that hinders you from engaging in anything difficult and valuable. It's the voice that stops you from doing something great simply because you may not succeed, and you may become embarrassed when you fail. It's the same voice that's telling you not to be vulnerable and open up your heart to find true love. The moment you identify your fears, then I believe you will have the courage to face them with strength as well as the support of your partner.

Most soon-to-be dads, especially first-time dads, experience different kinds of reactions when they are about to become a parent. This ranges from the excitement that they are about to be dads, to the fear of being a new dad. Unfortunately, the inner world of dads is similar – we hardly discuss it. Well, as the big day approaches, feeling anxious and fearful about possible changes that might take place in your life and being stressed is pretty common. In fact, the sleepless nights that will follow after the arrival of your baby is enough to make an expectant dad worried. So, what are some of the common fears of fatherhood that you're experiencing? We shall be looking at some of the commonest ones. I believe you can subdue all the fears in you and enjoy one of the most satisfying things any man can ever have – a gift of life. Some of these fears are not difficult to deal with while others are simply a matter of perception and attitude, and they require small adaptations that will provide great benefits in the end. Let's go through the top worries that are common among new dads and don't forget that you're definitely not alone if you're always worried about being a dad – a good number of expectant dads are also dealing with the same type of fear.

Will something Terrible happen?

This is one of the most common fears that men have when their partner is pregnant. What if there are challenges with the health of the baby? What if their partner experiences birth complications? Well, asking a lot of *"what if"* questions in times like this are completely normal, especially when something as big as expecting a new baby is going to happen soon. Although this is how our brains handle uncertain situations, it's crucial to also keep things in perspective. One of the things you can do to ease off the pressure of anything going wrong with the delivery or baby is by speaking to your doctor regarding the concerns you have. You can easily re-align your thinking and remember what differentiates the things that are "probable" and the things that are technically possible. By having this kind of information, you will be able to silence the fearful thoughts whenever they show up and concentrate more on the things you can control such as how you can support your partner when the big day comes or your birth plan.

I hope I will be a Good Dad

Another common fear that first-time soon-to-be dads experience is having the inner thoughts of whether they will be good dads. The truth is that there are a lot of sacrifices involved when men move from a young partnered or married adult into playing the role of a father. A new father needs a lot of wisdom to help mold their child into a responsible adult. Well, it's also important to bear in mind that you have the choice to be a good father. So, go ahead and learn as much as you can about good fatherhood and following the examples of other dads will help you learn better. You may have to give up on several activities and follow up on learning the principles of effective fathering. If there are great children close to you whose dads played an excellent role in making sure they become great kids, then you can do it.

Can I handle the cost of a new baby?

The truth is that babies often bring a lot of costs – expenses on clothing as well as disposable diapers and several others. If you're a first-time expectant father, then these costs may likely appear as new to you and even to your partner. However, it' possible to handle baby expenses by carrying out careful budgeting and being creative. Well, you'll also need to make some sacrifices too, but don't forget that any sacrifice you're making is for the good of your child. Isn't it better to sacrifice for your child than to sacrifice for other things that are not so important to you?

How can I keep the Baby Safe?

When you're faced with the responsibility of taking care of a delicate life of your baby who can't even care for himself, the question that comes to mind is, can I really take care of the child safely? New babies are delicate and as a father, you'll have to hold the baby correctly, put on the diaper the right way and ensure that the stroller or crib is safe enough. Also, don't forget that you need to babyproof your home; all these things are enough reasons to be afraid. Fortunately, you can deal with most of these fears through education. For instance, you can start practicing before your baby is born, especially if your friend or neighbor has a new baby. Learn how to hold a baby and ask questions about safe baby furniture as well as other information you need. If this is making you get very nervous, why don't you learn to babysit a new-born with your partner for a friend? It's a low-risk chance to practice and get some experience.

Divided Attention and Love

Another area of concern for expectant dads is the issue of possible changes in the relationship between you and your partner as you become parents. Well, your partner has been your playmate for some time now, but her role is likely going to change now since she will be your child's mother too. Well, if you're worried that your wife may love your baby more than you, then you have to stop worrying because she will undoubtedly love both of you. However, it's also crucial to understand that as a mother, her attention may shift more to your baby because a new-born often requires much attention after birth – this will require her energy, attention and body. So, if the duration of time you spend alone with your spouse is how you measure love, then I suggest you search for other ways to measure it. The truth is that as you team up with your partner to raise your child properly, you will discover that your feelings and love for each other will even deepen more than ever before.

New baby and Your Sex life

You may find it disturbing to think that when your baby is finally born, your partner may not be ready for sex immediately. Well, I guess you must have even started experiencing some of these changes in her while she's pregnant. This is also related to not spending enough time with your partner after the birth of your baby. Remember, the little time you may lose now or how much you're missing your sex life is only temporary. With time, things will be back to normal and you may even experience a new and better level of physical and emotional intimacy with your partner. Later in the next chapter, we shall also be looking at how to enhance your sex drive, which may be affected by couvade symptoms.

Will having a new baby stop me from enjoying the things I love?

You may be wondering whether the birth of your child may prevent you from enjoying the things you love doing. This kind of fear is prevalent among first-time dads, and the question on your mind may be; *"Will my life be over when my child is born?"* Undoubtedly, having a child is a big commitment, but you're not alone because a lot of men experience this fear also. One of the worries is that as soon as the child is born, then you won't be as adventurous and spontaneous as before. You feel that you may never be able to take risks like before and that once you have a child, then you will end up giving up all the hobbies and activities you love and enjoy. Fathers who have this fear feel that having a child implies that they have to sacrifice their dreams or may be put them on hold. The truth is that every child is different and each child will always enhance your life differently. What are the kind of activities you love? Do you enjoy dancing, skiing, singing, mountain climbing? What are your favorite activities? Did you know that you can make your partner and kids your fans? I believe your partner and kids would love to see you perform. So, if you genuinely love something, then there is nothing wrong in sharing it with your family. It even gets better when you explore your partner's interests as well as that of your kids as they grow up. Many fathers explore incredible adventures with their partner while others do so with their children. There is no doubt that children will add a new element of responsibility. This often requires you to spend extra time making plans before executing what you want to do.

Well, the trade-off is always worth every extra effort you make. It takes faith to become a father and the opposite of fear is faith. It takes a lot of faith as a father to see the value of a precious little baby who will stare at you with pure love for willing to put aside all your concerns and fears and take up this responsibility of a father.

How Soon-to-be Dads Can Lose "Baby Weight."

The truth is that among the symptoms of couvade syndrome earlier discussed, weight gain is the most understandable side effect that expectant dads experience. Interestingly, getting off the extra weight is also relatively easy. According to a UK study, it was discovered that on average, soon-to-be dads added extra 14 pounds in the course of their partner's pregnancy. We've earlier discussed some of the possible explanations for "baby weight" such as snacking sympathy, more dining out before the delivery of their baby and bigger meals at home. The main issue with the weight gain most expectant dads experience is that once your baby is born, you often become too busy to even think about the food you eat and the need for regular exercise. Unfortunately, this ends up causing the weight gain to stay on and possibly affect the health of soon-to-be dads. I know that the last thing that a dad would even consider while preparing for his baby is the extra pounds. According to a 2015 study which studied 10,000 men for 20 years, it was observed that fathers who had children were even more likely to add an average of 4 pounds. This explains why it's crucial to have the willpower to take steps to do what is needed to get rid of the excess weight even before the birth of the baby. Are you an expectant father and you're wondering how to eliminate the extra weight that has accumulated courtesy of couvade syndrome? You don't have to worry anymore because I shall be sharing several tips to help you deal with it.

When you search for *"How do I lose weight"* on Google, you'll be amazed to find out that the phrase has been typed about 150,000 or more each month. Well, the problem here is that most of the answers you will find are often ridiculous weight loss ideas that fail to clearly explain what men with symptoms of couvade syndrome need to do to lose weight and keep the weight away from their lives. Actually, another problem with most of the content out there is that they tend to conflict with one another, and this leads to more confusion than good results. I'm not disputing the fact that you can lose weight by adopting different strategies such as vegetarian, intermittent fasting, paleo or low-carb diets. Interestingly, you can also lose weight by not doing anything special other than eating a moderate amount of good food. To enjoy sustainable physical transformation, you have to make healthy alterations to the kind of diet you eat, effectively control your total calories intake and engage in regular exercise. I also know that other approaches might work in the short-term, but most of the results don't last. As a soon-to-be dad, you can lose weight by following these steps (specially created for men dealing with couvade syndrome), which I'll be discussing shortly. It's actually possible for you to lose as much as 12 kilos with six weeks but perhaps the only way you can achieve such results is by hunger strike. If you genuinely desire to get rid of fat instead of muscle and avoid stopping your metabolism; if you want to avoid cases of fat rebound (gaining lard almost the same day you stop dieting) and become healthier instead of almost decomposing in a bid to lose weight, then I would suggest that you aim for one kilo each week.

Losing "Baby Weight" Without Losing your Muscle Mass

For men, the answer to the popular question "how to lose weight" is often a wrong one. When you begin to add weight as an expectant dad, your focus should be on "how you can get rid of fat while retaining or even increasing fat-free mass. By fat-free mass, I mean the organs, connective tissue, muscles, bones as well as water weight. These are the things that you have left after removing every trace of fat cell from your body. Experts have observed that new dads usually accumulate extra pound around their lower back and mid-sections. Naturally, men have muscles in their legs, arms and chests and these muscles often stay longer even without having to work out. The reason for this is that men tend to exercise these areas daily while carrying out their activities. You should understand that the major component of your fat-free mass is your muscle mass. So, it's crucial for our muscle mass to weigh more than our fat mass.

In fact, one of the benefits of having a good muscle mass is that it has a tremendous impact on your metabolic rate or metabolism. In case you're unsure what that means, metabolic rate has to do with the level of calories your body can burn for energy. When you have more muscle mass, then you also increase the calories you burn even during periods you're not engaging in physical activities. But what will also help you go through this activity is the muscle mass – whether in life or gym. The muscle mass plays a crucial role in maintaining a healthy weight and in your weight loss efforts. It helps to strengthen and support the joints, improves balance and even helps you to lower the risk of injury significantly. So, as we examine various ways to lose weight and regain your perfect shape before the symptoms of couvade syndrome kicked in, you should always remember that holding onto your muscle mass is a high priority even when you're dieting.

Eating for Weight Loss

Although there has been an increase in the number of people who go on a diet, we can easily conclude that the success rate of most diet is low because the rate of obesity is still on the increase. So, to get rid of baby weight, we shall be taking a different approach because the word "diet" gives people the mindset that it's just for a short time. This explains why experts in the field and nutritionists usually warn that extreme restriction of calorie intake (dieting) isn't the best solution. It's possible to get the short-term results, but as you continue to under eat, you'll only end up feeling awful and find it even harder to engage in your workouts. Getting rid of baby weight requires a different approach which is better than just eating less. The starting point is to examine the way you think. While you enjoyed snacking along with your pregnant wife, you must begin to avoid seeing food as something to limit in a bid to lose weight. Instead, you have to think differently and see food as the fuel needed by your body to stay healthy. Food should be what you consume for the kind of healthy lifestyle you desire. So, you can make the changes to your mindset simply by replacing all the sugary drinks or high-calorie drinks with the ones having zero-calories. Alternatively, you can lower the amount of high-calorie liquids you take.

The second thing you need to do is to come up with a plan on how to curb your intake of a specific *"problem meal"* where you tend to either overeat or consume junk food instead of healthy foods that are filled with nutrients such as whole grains and low-fat protein. Are you having issues with lunch? Maybe your wife is unable to pack your lunch because of your baby, or perhaps you're often tempted to eat out simply because most of your colleagues love to do so. It could even be dinner or breakfast. Regardless of the meal which poses as your greatest challenge, you can make tremendous progress in your efforts to get rid of baby weight by simply fixing this little problem. Interestingly, it even gets better because it doesn't require much work when compared to attempting to fix every meal at the same time. In fact, you can make a big difference by prioritizing protein in any meal that was initially empty calories.

It's important to understand where you are right now before you start cutting down on your calories. You can achieve this by monitoring the way you eat. When you track your nutrition, you no longer see portions as something you're served, but as decisions. It will also help you discover all the "hidden calories" in your diet which you might have overlooked if you didn't track your nutrition. Did you know that this alone can help you make significant progress? The reason why you should take note of the numbers is that most of us tend to underestimate, overestimate and in some cases, flat-out lie regarding how much exercise we do and our real weight. In fact, sometimes, we don't even realize that we're doing it. So, go ahead and identify your daily calorie target and then you can continue to monitor it to help you ascertain whether to adjust your intake of calories. One more thing you need to know is that it's possible to get rid of baby weight and live a healthy life. But you have to make the healthy habits I'll be sharing below a permanent aspect of your life.

1. *Endeavour to take your Breakfasts*

Did you know that a study which was published in the US journal Obesity Research revealed that three out of four individuals who successfully get rid of a significant amount of weight (and successfully keep it off) take their breakfast every morning? Well, it's an indication that eating a well-chosen breakfast early in the morning helps to boost your metabolic rate. It also helps to lower your risk of making poor choices of food for the rest of the day or even overeating. So, remember to take into consideration the kind of healthy food you need to eat – low-carb, protein, fibers and several others.

2. *Increase the Nutrient Density of your Foods*

Another word for this could be *"food efficiency,"* and it's undoubtedly among the best ways to increase your nutrition per calorie you eat. This helps also to ensure that you remain satisfied for a longer time and quickly fills you up while providing all the required nutrients with fewer calories. By eating food that's nutritionally balanced – with healthy fats, fresh fruits, protein, non-starchy vegetables, and unprocessed carbohydrates, then the food you eat will digest slowly. This, in turn, will help to maintain an excellent blood-sugar level in your body. The reason why you may have an increase in your *"hunger signals"* is that there is a reduction in your blood glucose levels. You can set aside some time in the evening to create a menu because it will be a bit difficult to do this while you're getting ready for work in the morning.

3. *Be Deliberate about your Snacks*

It's often easy for you to be tempted by junk foods when you feel your stomach rumbling while you're far from home. The chances of yielding is high unless you've planned. So, you have to anticipate hunger pangs during the day and make provision for nutritious snacks like whole-grain cereal bars and dried fruits. Don't forget to include a little healthy fat to ensure that you keep the hunger pangs away.

4. *Avoid Trans Fat*

The truth is that your body truly needs fat and is capable of burning fat except one – trans-fat. Unfortunately, whenever you eat or snack on fried foods as well as some processed baked foods, you're increasing your intake of trans-fat. If you genuinely want to regain your weight, shape, and improve your heart health after the birth of your baby, then you need to stay away from partially hydrogenated vegetable oil. Are you searching for a healthy way to give yourself a treat? Well, you're better off consuming just a piece of chocolate (mainly because it has anti-oxidants) than preparing your entire meals with food items that add no value to your health.

5. *Embrace Healthy Eating*

Eating the right amount of calories based on your level of activeness is the key to a healthy diet. It helps you to balance your energy consumption with the energy you utilize each day. One of the things that lead to weight gain is when you eat or drink more than your body requires since the excess energy will end up being stored as fat. This is simply the reason why you lose weight when you drink or eat too little. To get a balanced diet and ensure that your body gets all the nutrients it requires, you have to eat a wide range of foods. Experts recommend that men should have a daily calorie intake of 2,500 calories while women are advised to have about 2,000 calories daily. This also applies to soon-to-be dads who may be adding weight, especially in their waist region and stomach. Other tips to help you eat healthily include:

- **Focus on eating more starchy carbohydrates and fiber -** Endeavour to add at least one starchy food to your main meal each day and eat more wholegrain or higher fiber varieties such as brown rice, whole wheat, or potatoes with their skins on.

- **Fruits and vegetables are essential** - Experts also recommend that we should eat a minimum of five portions of a variety of vegetable and fruits daily. The fruits can be canned, juiced, fresh, dried or frozen. It's not really difficult to achieve the five portions of fruits and veg each day. You can swap your regular mid-morning snack for fresh fruits or slice a banana and add to your cereal for breakfast.

- **Fish and oily fish** - Apart from being an excellent source of protein; fish also provides vitamins and minerals. In addition, oily fish will provide you with omega-3 fats and this is good for your heart health. Strive to eat a minimum of two portions of fish weekly in addition to a portion of oily fish such as herring, mackerel, salmon, pilchards and trout. Examples of non-oily fish you can eat include tuna, hake, haddock, skate, cod and plaice.

6. *Lower your Intake of Sugar and Saturated Fat*

Remember, I earlier explained that you need to choose the right kind of fat. Fat is essential to your diet; however, you also need to be careful of the amount as well as the type of fat you're eating. Generally, fat is of two kinds; unsaturated and saturated fat. When you consume more saturated fat, it might increase the amount of cholesterol in your blood, and this will, in turn, increase your risk of developing heart disease. For men, the recommended amount of saturated fat is 30g and examples of food with saturated fat are:

- Cakes
- Pies
- Butter
- Fatty cuts of meat
- Biscuits
- Sausages
- Cream
- Lard

- Butter
- Hard cheese

Your focus should be on unsaturated fat and choose lean cuts when having meat and try to cut off any fat you notice on it. You increase your risk of obesity as well as tooth decay by consuming foods or drinks with high sugar content. This means that you need to stay away from most packaged foods and beverages such as sugary breakfast cereals, sweets and chocolate, sugary fizzy drinks and alcoholic drinks. One easy way to identify the amount of sugar in a drink or food is to check its food label.

7. *Reduce your Salt Intake*

Remember, one of the common symptoms of couvade syndrome is anxiety and excess consumption of salt can increase your blood pressure. You may not be adding too much salt to your food, but that doesn't imply that you're not eating too much salt. A good portion of the salt you eat comes from the ones added to the foods you buy like bread, sauces, cereals and soups. To check the amount of salt in what you're buying, you can check food labels.

8. *Stay Hydrated*

The best way to stay hydrated is to take lots of fluids. Generally, experts recommend that we take 6-8 glasses of water each day in addition to the fluids in the food we eat. Although the water from non-alcoholic drinks also counts, the healthier choices are the ones you get from coffee, tea, lower-fat milk and lower sugar drinks. The quantity of water you drink may likely increase when the weather is hot, and several factors could either increase or slightly reduce the amount of your daily water intake. For instance, you tend to drink more water when you engage in physical activities, and the opposite may also apply.

Cooking Tips

One of your focus when getting rid of baby weight is to maintain or even build muscle. To achieve this, you need to have a perfect combination of diet and exercise. You can achieve the right weight and muscle mass by practicing the tips earlier shared with you and adding healthy weight loss foods with "smart cooking" methods. So, here are some smart ways to cook your meals to keep them lean:

- **Learn to grill:** Do you love a good steak? You can still enjoy your favorite steak in your diet as long as you grill it without extra butter or oil. This is because most of the beef you're eating already contains sufficient fat, so why add more? If you want to grill lean poultry, consider drizzling with a small amount of olive oil. This will increase your intake of healthy fats.
- **Poach:** Did you know that many experienced cooks poach seafood? It helps them maximize flavor and also helps to lower the level of added fat required to prepare the food. So, if you want to poach salmon, you can simmer about an inch of liquid on your stovetop. Then add the fish in your warm water and allow to cook as desired.

- **Roast:** One of the best ways to bring out the savory flavor of vegetables is roasting. In fact, it's one of the easiest methods of cooking our foods. You can slice your onions, carrots, Brussels sprouts or vegetables and drizzle with a little amount of olive oil. Season with pepper, herbs and salt as desired and place in the oven at about 400 degrees. Roasting remains a healthy and smart way to prepare healthy meals.
- **Sautee:** You can lighten up your favorite meal and sauté instead of frying it. With this method, you end up using less oil and still enjoy the flavor of your fish, veggies and meat.

Tips for Choosing Meals

When trying to get rid of baby weight, you need to choose whole foods such as lean protein, fruits, healthy fats and vegetables as earlier mentioned. This provides you with sufficient fiber as well as water and a lower intake of calories. Consider changing from higher-fat protein foods to lean types since they can help you keep satiety while reducing your overall consumption. If you're thinking of specific foods to buy, here is a list of some weight loss foods:

- Poultry such as turkey breast, chicken (you can reduce the fat content by selecting the skinless ones)
- Low-fat Greek yogurt (choose brands with a lower level of sugar)
- Lean cuts of beef like flank steak or filet mignon
- Fish (you can refer to the list of healthy fish I earlier shared) but remember, your focus should be more on fish with "good fat."

- Bison as well as other game meats that are flavorful and lean
- Healthy beans such as black-eyed peas, black beans and chickpeas
- Fresh fruits which can satisfy your sweet tooth
- Cottage cheese (make sure you lookout for the sodium content which you can always find on the nutrition label, especially for those monitoring their salt level)
- Dark green leafy vegetables such as broccoli or kale
- Whole grains such as brown rice, quinoa, buckwheat, and barley

Exercise

Being deliberate about the kind of food you eat is important, but you also need to exercise regularly. Just like most dads, you may work all day and as soon as you're home, you want to spend as much time as possible with the baby. Well, this ends up distracting you from going to the gym or working out. This is why most dads find it difficult to get rid of the fat they accumulated as a result of sympathetic pregnancy. Just like most mothers who need to work out to maintain a flat stomach and shape after delivery, men need to be deliberate about getting back to shape after baby weight. But when it comes to what works for expectant dads, it may be a bit different from most of the tips out there. For instance, it's easy for people to tell you to hit the gym and sweat it out every day or spend hours with the treadmill or elliptical. The truth is that this shouldn't always be the case, especially for soon-to-be dads. It's often better to start with activities that you love, especially if you're new to the exercise world. You could start by just running, hiking or playing soccer with friends – anything that can keep you active for at least 60 minutes each day for 3-4 times each week. This will give you a good feeling about yourself as you experience some success. But as you engage in these activities, you can now begin to add more structured training which I will be sharing with you shortly.

For soon-to-be dads, focusing on structured training like cardio and strength training, especially like high-intensity interval training, is crucial. Remember, we earlier talked about muscle mass, and one of the best ways to build muscle mass is to engage in strength training exercises. Let's go through some examples of exercise you can do to get rid of baby weight.

12 Exercises to help Work off Baby Weight

Here are some activities you can do to help you work off the weight you gained courtesy of couvade.

1. *Drills*

This should be the first workout you need to do. It should serve as a test to help you determine how fit you are and to help you know how you can make improvements. So, begin with this sequence and find out how many you can complete in a minute. Go ahead and do four push-ups, then eight counts of mountain climbers. Next, jump up and make sure that the palms of your hand touch your knees. Stand up straight, then move your arms up together to your head and drop back down to a plank position and repeat the entire movements. You will be able to do more as you progress with these movements.

2. Power Knee

Begin this exercise by planting your feet a bit wider than your hips. Then spread your arms to the right side and bring your hands together. Lift your left knee up and move your hands to the knee you lifted. Next, extend your arms back up to full extension while your hand should be brought to your lifted knee. Go ahead and extend your arms back up to full extension then your left knee should be brought down to its original position. Make sure that you keep your right foot firm with your core tight. Then repeat the entire process but this time on the opposite side and alternate.

3. Plank Punches

Begin this exercise in a plank position, then bring one arm extended with a closed fist. Next, you can alternate your hands and do this in a punching motion. You can achieve this by bringing your arm up, then extend it in front of you (straight) and in line with your body. You can now lower your hand under your shoulder, then proceed to switch hands.

4. Ski-Abs

Start this exercise in an excellent plank position while making sure you keep your feet together. Then begin by moving your knee towards your left hand to the point that your left elbow almost touches your knees.

Then return your feet to its starting position and extend your legs outwards. You can now repeat the whole movement and alternate.

5. Suicide Drills

To do this exercise, you will require some space. So go ahead and shuffle to one side, then drop into a wide squat while touching the floor with the opposite hand. You will be able to touch the floor with your left hand (after your squat) if you're shuffling properly.

6. Low Plank Oblique

Begin with a plank position raising your right leg. Now using your core and obliques, move your right knee towards your right elbow and if you can, make contact. Next, bring back your right leg to the starting position, then do the same with your left leg and repeat.

7. Moving Push-Ups

Begin with a push-up and make sure your feet are spread out a bit wider than your hips. Move your body to one side while maintaining your plank position, then bring your feet and hands together. Keep moving in the same direction and move your back out to hip-width and also bring your hands to your sides for another push-up. Make sure you repeat until there is no more room, then proceed in the other direction.

8. *Power Squats*

Just like a jumping jack, go ahead and spread your legs a bit wider than your shoulder-width then bend at your knees as you assume a squat position. To jump back up into your starting position, push from the heels. Ensure that your knees do not pass your toes when performing this move.

9. *Strength Training*

It's easy for you to conclude that strength training exercises such as weight lifting are only meant for bodybuilding or for getting huge. But if you genuinely want a lasting weight control that will also give you back the perfect shape you've been dreaming of, then you need to engage in strength training. The primary reason why you need to engage in a strength training exercise is that as I earlier explained, muscle tissue usually burns more calories than fat. In fact, the more muscle tissue you have, the more you'll burn.

Don't forget that muscle tissue has other advantages; it not only gives you more control over your health; it also enhances your appearance in ways that simple calorie control can't. In addition, it enables you to develop the strength and energy required to handle most of your daily activities. Interestingly, you can approach strength training in different ways; it could be through a bodybuilding-style, high or low reps, and several others. If fat loss is your goal, then I would suggest that you consider full-body training.

Weight Training

This is also a great way to start if you haven't been exercising at all because the last thing you want to do is to stress your body too much. Here is an excellent starter exercise plan for men. You can do the following for three days in a week and make sure you leave at least one day in between.

- Practice bodyweight exercises and rotate between push-ups, lunges, squats, crunches, leg-lifts and pullups.
- To start, practice five reps of each exercise and before moving onto the next exercise, have a break of 15 seconds in between each exercise.
- Continue to rotate for about 20 minutes.
- In case you're finding it hard to do full push-ups, consider doing modified push-ups off the wall at an angle. You can even do it on your knees. You can also grab a chair to help you keep your feet on if you can't do full pull-ups just like most guys at first.
- You can give yourself a break if you're unable to complete the entire 20 minutes. Ensure that you're continually improving your workout as you move forward in the starter exercise plan.

10. Cardio and HIIT

What often comes to mind when you hear the word cardio is a treadmill, but that's just one of the options you have to get it done. Among the most effective weight-loss tools you can use is high-intensity interval training

(HIIT). One of the advantages of HIIT is that you can easily incorporate it into any fitness plan of your choice. This is because you can apply it to several settings as well as various kinds of equipment.

Here is a plan for cardio exercises. For five days in a week, make sure you do the following:

- Go for a walk for 30 minutes and during your walks, use a medium to high-intensity walking and remember, there is no need looking like a weird power walker. All you need to do is to keep your pace up as you walk.
- While walking during the day, you can actually split up your walking. For instance, you can take a 15-minute break in the morning and afternoon or walk for 15 minutes in the morning and night.

During your off days, between your body-weight sets three days each week, practice the following:

- For a total of 12-15 minutes, practice high-intensity intervals. This includes a 1-2 minutes-walk or light running and sprinting for about 30-45 seconds.

The table below is a 15 minutes high-intensity interval plan which makes it easy for you to understand.

Time Interval	Activity
2 ½ minutes	Warmup, light walking to running

45 seconds	Sprint
1 minute	Light running
45 seconds	Sprint
1 minute	Engage in light running
45 seconds	Sprint
1 minute	Light running
45 seconds	Sprint
1½ minute	Practice light running
30 seconds	Sprint
1½ minute	Light running
30 seconds	Sprint
2½ minutes	Calm down a bit, then do light running to walking

Do all the exercises for about three weeks and observe a "light" week. During this light week, you can engage in cardio to enable you to overcome a possible plateau often experienced after about one month, and it will enable you to give your body rest after engaging in bodyweight exercises. You will find the exercises easier as you move forward and you can even add light dumbbells or more reps.

When it comes to weight loss for men, the primary focus is to make sure that you eat a sustainable and tasty diet while making sure that your exercise remains challenging and fun. I believe that you can lose weight simply by making changes to your diet, but if you genuinely desire to drastically get rid of fat, retain muscle mass and get rid of baby weight and fat in your waistline, then you need to add the exercises I just shared.

Chapter IV

Dealing with Stress, Anxiety & Gastrointestinal Symptoms

Managing the Stress and Anxiety of Expectant Dads

As I earlier pointed out, expecting a new child can be a source of joy and also stress. By learning to handle most of the difficult emotions and issues that you face, you will end up developing a rewarding relationship with your child. The truth is that the effects of becoming a father can never be underestimated even though men sometimes don't show outward signs to prove it. In some cases, new dads may even be astonished not because of how proud they are of their partner or how beautiful their baby is, but by the shock of seeing how helpless the new-born is.

Tips to Help you Deal with Stress and Anxiety

We've earlier seen some of the reasons why soon-to-be dads fear when expecting a child. However, most guys have issues discussing some of their fears or coping with them, and this ends up leading to anxiety and stress. As soon as you've enjoyed the excitement of being a father when you discovered that your partner is pregnant, you may gradually become anxious about what the future holds. Several things could be the cause of stress for expectant dads who may be experiencing anxiety which is part of the symptoms of couvade syndrome. The first thing you need to do is to identify the causes of stress in your life. We've earlier seen some of the things that expectant fathers are afraid of; they are the leading causes of anxiety. First, identify these causes of stress and bear in mind that even though there is no prize for your efforts, you're doing it for your child. So, here are some tips to help you deal with the anxiety of being a new dad and dealing with one of the most prevalent symptoms of sympathetic pregnancy.

Paternity Leave

Perhaps the thought of asking to take time off from work is one of the commonest sources of anxiety and stress for expectant dads. If you're in this position, then know that you're not alone. The reason is that as parents, you have the strong urge to stay home and look after your wife and baby after birth which unfortunately collides with your strong anxieties about your finances. Bills will undoubtedly increase and not working leaves you with less funds to pay bills while having a new addition to your home. It's advisable to speak with your employer as early as you can if you and your wife agree that you need to take some time off. Of course, it's not a good idea to approach your boss one early morning to break the news that your wife is in labor and you may not be coming to work for the next three months. It's also crucial that you don't go to your employer's office trying to tell him what the law states about paternity leave. Telling your boss what your rights are while trying to request for leave isn't a good idea. Preferably, you can offer suggestions on how to remain useful to the company while staying with your wife and baby when they need you. For instance, is it possible to work from a home office? If yes, then you can go ahead and make that suggestion. When you resolve the issue of leave with your boss as early as possible, then you'll feel more in control.

Seek Social Support

The first question you need to ask yourself right now is, are you the first person to feel the way you're feeling right now? Of course, the answer is no! Ignoring major stress and anxiety in your life isn't really manly. What's more manly here is realizing the issues you're having as an expectant father and facing them head-on. So, go ahead and bond with other fathers to get the social support and tips required to overcome the anxiety. You can join groups on social media like Facebook or other websites where fellow fathers socialize. Meeting with other dads isn't an avenue to commiserate with each other; it's a time to interact with other guys experiencing the same issues you're facing.

Have a Me-Time

It's easy for an expectant dad to fall into the trap of being present at all times before qualifying to be a "dad." Unfortunately, this is a wrong precedent to set because it often leads to burnout. The best option is to create time to reset. Unfortunately, life lacks a pause button just like video games; however, spending as little as 30 minutes or one hour every week alone will serve as a reset button. This is even more important for the "stay-at-home dads" who are always surrounded by their children daily. This, in my opinion, is the closest thing to pressing the reset button

You have to be more involved

Undoubtedly, this may appear to be counterintuitive; however, the truth is that it's often tricky for expectant fathers, especially, first-time dads to establish a connection to the newest member of their home. This usually leads to stress and anxiety as they attempt to discover how to become a more active member of the house. While you may not feel involved during your partner's pregnancy since you're not always reminded of the pregnancy like your partner, you can also get involved in other ways. For instance, you can always place your hands on your partner's baby bump and feel your baby kick. Discussing the pregnancy with other people can also help you get involved and don't forget to sing, read or talk near your partner's belly; this is an easy way for your baby to recognize your voice after birth. You can also attend prenatal classes with your partner to ensure you know what you're likely going to expect during delivery and get a few tips on how to care for a new-born. During the early days after delivery, most of the responsibility rests on your partner, especially if she opts to breastfeed your baby. This makes you as a father to appear as a mere spectator in the game while your partner gets all the attention. Your self-worth as a new dad will get a boost when you simply add more responsibility to yourself. So, go ahead and identify new ways to become more involved – it could be to feed your baby from the bottle while your spouse is busy pumping the milk.

Overcome Loneliness by Preparing for Fatherhood

Your partner will undoubtedly become very busy with several activities – urinating almost every 15 minutes or less or selecting maternity clothes. But I believe that the best way to overcome the loneliness associated with being an expectant dad is to prepare for fatherhood. The truth is that whether you're still trying to deal with the symptoms of couvade syndrome or the shock of the fact that what you've been waiting for several years ago is about to happen; being an expectant dad is often a defining moment. But having a mixture of feelings it's perfectly normal – having the feelings of joy with outright horror of what awaits you in less than nine months – even when it was what you've always desired. It's often hard to be completely ready to become a dad and deal with symptoms of sympathetic pregnancy, but you can overcome the loneliness by preparing for fatherhood. Here are some tips to guide you as you prepare to welcome your baby into your home.

1. Research

Although you may not be the one physically carrying the baby, you're as involved as your spouse, especially with some of the symptoms of couvade syndrome you're having. Even though you're not physically pregnant, it doesn't prevent you from being a part of the birth experience. You'll find lots of books that have been written for expectant dads useful and reading this book is actually one of the best ways to overcome your fears, worries and loneliness. For instance, you can help your partner who may be experiencing several pregnancy symptoms such as heartburn, morning sickness and several others by researching on the subject. Having a better understanding of what your partner is feeling is an excellent way to support her better as she carries your baby. You also need to know what to expect after the birth of your child and this information will help to reduce your fears and worries about the entire process. Other things you can read about include types of deliveries such as caesarean and vaginal deliveries. Understand more about diaper changing, breastfeeding and several others.

2. *Keep Fit and be Healthy*

Earlier, I shared some of the ways to eat healthily and keep fit. Perhaps the best time to focus on your health is before the arrival of your baby. For instance, if you smoke, then consider quitting because there is evidence to suggest that smoking during pregnancy might increase the risk of congenital heart defects in new-borns. You can benefit a lot from the tips on healthy eating earlier shared.

3. *Discuss Parenting with your Partner*

Another excellent way to overcome the feeling of loneliness is to take advantage of the time before delivery to discuss parenting with your partner. What's your opinion about breastfeeding? Share your opinion with your partner. What about the crib; do you want your baby to sleep in a separate room after birth or in a crib? What plans do you have for childcare? If you're a first-time expectant dad, then these things may appear strange to both of you. Breastfeeding may actually pose as a bigger challenge than you thought and such issues need to be addressed. Even though you may talk about things that may not sound relevant, discussing with your partner helps ensure that you're more involved and not lonely. Other topics you can talk about include child discipline and how to cope when your baby becomes a feisty toddler. Such discussions will always keep the communication lines open between you and your spouse.

4. Become a Team

This is the best time to begin to think of you and your partner as a team. Remember, you, your partner and baby are all connected for life whether your romantic relationship fails at some point. So, you need to let go of keeping scores as if you're competing with your partner. Begin to see things through the lens of letting go. If your partner feels exhausted or happens to be dealing with morning sickness (which you may also experience if you're experiencing couvade syndrome), then helping her out would be an excellent idea because you're also helping your baby in the process and yourself as well. Providing the food they need to eat at this point, handling some of the house chores and checking in on them daily will always prove your support for a common purpose – taking care of your family.

5. *What kind of Dad do you want to be?*

The best time to make up your mind on the kind of father you want to be is before the birth of your baby. You may be lucky enough to have a great dad of your own, which means that you will love to be like him and that's fantastic. What if your father didn't leave so much to be desired? This is an excellent reason to become nervous whenever you think of your role as a father. Well, you're free to choose the kind of approach you would embrace a father. Go ahead and identify some excellent fatherhood role models and understand that you're actually creating this role from the start, so how you want it to look is purely your choice to make.

You can check out my other book *"Soon To Be DAD: Handbook For Expectant Fathers"* (ASIN: B088FP8JRW) for more information. You will certainly find excellent tips on how to be an excellent father.

Relieving Stress and Anxiety with meditation

Another way to effectively reduce stress is through meditation. Meditation helps you to maintain a healthy lifestyle, and you don't have to be experienced in it before you practice it. Once you consistently practice meditation, it gradually becomes easy to maintain. Since it's one way to build resilience to stress, this should be one of the best ways to handle your couvade symptoms as well. I'll be sharing the steps to basic meditation practice.

Step 1. Secure a Comfortable Position

The starting point is to choose where and how you want to sit. Some people usually prefer sitting in a comfortable chair and others choose to sit cross-legged on the floor. Whichever position you choose, your goal should be to sit in a position that helps you to relax completely and still be awake – not the one that makes you sleep off. Also, you need to ensure that your posture is right. When you sit with your back straight, you find it easy to stay awake during your meditation. Having this in mind as you begin your meditation practice will ensure that your body gets used to the position even as you start practicing for more extended periods. If your preferred place to sit is a chair, then sit toward the front of the seat while positioning your feet firmly on the floor. With this, you will easily improve your posture and concentrate better.

Step 2. Gently Close your Eyes

Now that you're in a sitting position (whether on a chair or floor) and comfortable, gaze into the distance softly and gently lower your lids.

Your jaw needs to be slack and a bit open too. Your goal is to ensure that you relax all your facial muscles. Please, don't squeeze your eyes tight and if you notice that your face is tightened, you can slowly open your eyes, then gaze into the distance softly while lowering your eyes slowly. Now gradually begin to relax all other parts of your body and if you identify that some parts of your body are tensed, then take a deep breath and let it relax you.

Step 3. Set your thoughts Aside

I know you're worried about so many things, especially with the symptoms of couvade also affecting you, and it could be the thoughts of whether your partner and baby are doing well. Whatever be the cause of worry or your dominant thoughts, you have to put them aside. Undoubtedly, you may not be able to control your thoughts, but it's possible for you to control the level of power your thoughts have over you. I'm not suggesting that you ignore or suppress them; just remain calm and take note of your thoughts. Now, with your breathing, bring yourself back to the moment. Once you're able to do this while meditating, you can easily let go of things in your life too. There is every tendency that you may at this point get carried away in your thoughts, but you don't have to be too hard on yourself, especially if you're just doing it for the first time. Now take a moment to identify where your mind went off to without being judgmental and gradually return to your breathing.

Step 4. Keep going

Trust me, that's all you need to do. Just continue to put aside the thoughts that may enter into your mind, and as you do that, you will notice that the quiet spaces between such thoughts will continue to increase and continue as you practice for a longer time.

Now, this is just how to practice basic meditation and you may feel like you didn't get it right the first few times you try it, but that's perfectly okay. As you practice, you will begin to experience more consistency. Just bear in mind that meditation requires lots of practice and if you desire to be perfect in meditation, then you will only end up creating more stress than you eventually relieve. Trust me, there is no "perfect" meditation session anywhere and you will easily let yourself down by going into it with the belief that you will be perfect. Simply start with a short session which could last for five minutes and as soon as you become more comfortable, then increase the sessions to 10-15 minutes and continue until you can comfortably meditate for 30 minutes. This kind of meditation will become easier and more effective with practice, and you will always leave your meditation sessions feeling refreshed, relaxed and prepared to support your pregnant partner and baby.

One of the challenges that most people face when meditating is how to track time, especially when two minutes would seem like eternity while meditating. Remember, thoughts of whether you have reached the time to stop or not will only defeat the purpose of clearing your mind. So, instead of always thinking "how long have I meditated," you can simply use a timer. Most smartphones now come with a timer, so set the timer for the duration you want to meditate for each session. Make sure that the tone of the timer is a gentle one or you can set it to vibrate so that it doesn't end up startling you when time is up. Once you set the timer, remember to turn off your screen before you relax. The truth is that with time, you may even discover that you want to go even further and as you become comfortable and practice consistently, you can also skip the timer and spend more time meditating – as long as your body needs. What if you're not comfortable with this type of meditation? Then go for other types of meditation.

Dealing with Gastrointestinal Symptoms

One group of symptoms of sympathetic pregnancy that is quite common among soon-to-be dads are gastrointestinal symptoms, and we shall be looking at natural ways to deal with them in this section.

Heartburn

Sometimes, heartburn is also regarded as acid indigestion and it leads to a painful and burning feeling within the middle chest region of your body and in some cases, the upper part of your stomach. If you've not experienced this before and only began to experience it after your partner became pregnant, then chances are that it's a symptom of couvade syndrome. Apart from being one of the symptoms of sympathetic pregnancy, other things that could cause it include:

- Smoking
- Overeating
- stress

- The habit of lying down immediately after meals
- Taking caffeine or alcohol

Those who may experience it are people who are pregnant, smokers and overweight persons. Well, regardless of the cause of the heartburn, you can learn to avoid heartburn by avoiding some of the things people eat that further worsens the symptoms. For instance, the things that often trigger heartburn include:

- Coffee
- Alcohol
- Greasy foods
- Chocolate
- Onions
- Peppermint
- Fatty or fried foods
- Spicy foods
- Sodas as well as other bubbly drinks
- Tomatoes and tomato sauce
- Vinegar, salad dressings and hot sauces

Also, when you eat big meals, it can lead to heartburn, so, instead of having three heavy meals a day, consider taking several small meals during the day. Other things you can do to get rid of heartburn is to quit smoking if you smoke, especially when you're an expectant dad. If you're overweight, then it's recommended that getting rid of extra pounds (which usually exerts pressure on the stomach and forces excess acid up into your esophagus) should be reduced.

Enhancing your Digestive System

I earlier mentioned that if you haven't experienced any of these symptoms before, then you may be having symptoms of sympathetic pregnancy (if your partner is pregnant). There is no special way to treat gastrointestinal disease, but you can leverage the available treatments of such ailments. This includes the practice of good bowel habits and if you're over the age of 50, then consider a colonoscopy. You should bear in mind that apart from possibly being a symptom of couvade syndrome, your lifestyle as well as the type of foods you eat and directly impacts your digestive health. So, regardless of the cause, you can take the steps below to help you improve your digestive health and ensure that it functions efficiently while leading to a sense of well-being. Here are some tips to help with your gastrointestinal symptoms as you battle symptoms of couvade syndrome:

- **Increase your intake of fiber:** Nutrition experts believe that the consumption of foods that are high in fiber and also rich in whole grains, legumes, fruits and vegetables can significantly improve your digestive health. This is because foods that have high fiber content can help to keep the food you eat moving through your digestive tract. Consequently, this lowers the chances of getting constipated. High-fiber diets can also help in your weight loss efforts which is also one of the symptoms of couvade syndrome.

- **Don't just focus on fiber, but also on soluble and insoluble fiber:** It's not just enough to focus on fiber, you also need to eat both types because they can assist your digestive systems differently. For instance, insoluble fiber is the type that the body can't digest. I guess you may be wondering why you need to eat something that your body can't digest. There is nothing to worry because they help to add bulk to your stool. On the other hand, soluble fiber absorbs water which also stops you from having very watery stools. Examples of foods that contain insoluble fiber include vegetables, whole grains, and wheat bran while you can also get soluble fiber from seeds, legumes, nuts and oat bran.

- **Eat more of Lean meats:** We all know that a healthy diet must contain protein; however, fatty cuts of meat often causes uncomfortable digestion. So, it's better that when choosing meat, you should choose lean cuts like skinless poultry and pork loin.

- **Lower your intake of fatty foods:** Your digestive process tends to be affected when you eat fatty foods, and this causes you to experience constipation. Well, it's still important to add fatty foods to your diet to ensure a balanced diet, so, you can actually pair fatty foods with high-fiber foods to make them easier for your digestive system.

- **Always eat on schedule and remain hydrated:** Water is always good for your digestive health. The fiber you eat pulls water into the colon and ends up creating bulkier and softer stools, and this enables them to pass through with less stress. Also, by maintaining a regular schedule when you take your snacks and meals, you're actually ensuring that your digestive system is in top shape. So, remember to always sit down when taking breakfast, lunch, dinner as well as snacks around the same specific time daily.

- **Take more gut-friendly nutrients:** Another way to support your digestive tract is to eat more gut-supporting nutrients like probiotics. These are beneficial bacteria that may help to improve digestive health when you take them as supplements. Probiotics provide your gut with healthy bacteria that aids digestion by helping to break down indigestible fibers that if not broken down properly, may cause gas and bloating. You can find probiotics in fermented foods like kimchi, miso and yogurts. Other nutrients that support the guts include glutamine and zinc.

- **Endeavour to chew your food before swallowing:** Since the digestion of our food begins in the mouth, you need to be conscious of how you eat. You have to break down the foods you're eating into smaller pieces with your teeth to enable the enzymes found in your digestive tract to break down the food. Studies have revealed that there is a link between poor chewing of food and decreased nutrient absorption. You're actually giving your stomach less work to do when you chew your food thoroughly. It becomes easier for your stomach to turn the solid food you ate into a liquid mixture which finds it easier to enter your small intestine. Also, when you chew your food for a longer time, it leads to the production of saliva and more saliva is produced when you chew even longer. Interestingly, saliva helps to kickstart the digestion process in your mouth by simply breaking down some of the fats and carbohydrates in your meal. When the food you ate finally gets to your intestine, saliva also functions as a fluid that's mixed with solid food which ensures the smooth passage of the food into your intestines. Finally, thoroughly chewing your food provides sufficient saliva for digestion which may, in turn, prevent you from having some of the symptoms of heartburn and indigestion. In fact, you can even reduce stress by chewing your food and this may also help to improve indigestion.

- **Always exercise regularly:** When you exercise, it becomes easy for you to maintain a healthy weight and this is also good for your digestive health. Engaging in regular exercise usually helps to keep the foods moving through the digestive system and this is a great way to reduce constipation. So, always exercise; you can check out the section where I shared on exercise again to learn more.

Finally, learn to control your stress level. Among the common factors that can cause your digestive system to move into overdrive are stress and anxiety. One way to reduce your stress level is to engage in several stress-reducing activities regularly.

Coping with Pains and Aches

Leg and Muscle Cramps

While having other symptoms of couvade syndrome such as weight gain, one of the associated health challenges are leg cramps. You may experience this at night, even though it may not last for a very long time. They occur when your muscle contracts involuntarily on its own and this causes you to feel a strong lump at the point of pain which is the contracted muscle. There is always a reason why cramps occur and examining the possible causes is crucial. While you may feel that it's one of the symptoms of couvade syndrome, it's also a better option to confirm that there are no other possible causes of the leg cramps. For instance, if you've not strained a muscle, then it's likely you're experiencing the cramps because of fatigued muscles that you've overused or you're dehydrated. It's also possible that you're not getting sufficient electrolytes like magnesium and potassium and these are minerals that assist your muscles to work smoothly. In addition, fluids help your body to process the minerals. In the absence of any other underlying health issues that might be the cause; it is likely one of the symptoms of couvade, especially if you've not had it before. Regardless of the cause, majority of the cases of leg cramps don't really indicate the presence of a disturbing underlying health issue. Here are some of the best ways to ease off the problem of leg cramps and muscle cramps generally:

- **Stretch:** The first thing you need to do to relieve the cramp which could be leg cramps or other muscle cramps is to relax the cramping muscle. What's the activity that induced the cramp in the first place? Identify it and lightly stretch the muscle and gently hold the stretch. You can also massage the muscle as you stretch or when you're through stretching. If you're experiencing muscle cramps at night, you can slowly stand up and put weight on the part of your leg that is affected to push the heel down, then stretch out the muscle.

- **Hydration:** One of the ways to reduce leg cramps is to increase your intake of water. You may not get the relief from your cramps instantly, but as soon as you've become well hydrated or taken sufficient sports drinks with electrolytes, then you can easily prevent another cramp.

- **Apply Heat:** Some coaches and physical trainers often recommend that you use magnesium outside your body. This should be in the form of Epsom salts; so try applying this old remedy to a wet cloth. Then proceed to press it onto the areas of your cramped muscle. Alternatively, you can even add some to a hot bath and enjoy a soak. Interestingly, a hot soak is believed by many health experts to provide relief for several pains with or without Epsom salts. A heating pat is also another option, but not recommended for those who may have a spinal cord injury, diabetes or other conditions that may prevent you from feeling the heat.

- **Magnesium:** When you're often having leg cramps that are not in any way related to a more severe health issue, then consider adding more magnesium to the food you eat. Since magnesium has been suggested for treating pregnant women with muscle cramps (though more studies are required), you can take magnesium supplements, but talking to your doctor would be a better idea before taking it. Other excellent sources of magnesium include nuts and seeds.

Back pains

Another common symptom of couvade syndrome is back pain and it's also a common reason for missed workdays. The reason why the back is crucial is that our lower back supports the weight of the upper body, which includes the head, chest, stomach and waist region. Chances are that if you've added "baby weight," then you may also experience back pain. There are also other causes of lower back pain, such as an injury as well as the wear and tear of aging. Regardless of the cause of the lower back pain, some of the simple recommendations below can provide significant relief and even help to prevent future issues.

- **Stretch the muscles:** Just like leg cramps, stretching is an excellent way to relieve chronic as well as acute lower back pain. This will, in turn, prevent future lower back issues too. You need to engage in a variety of stretches because the muscles in the back spread to various directions in your body. Here are some of the basic lower back stretches you can do:
  - You can lie flat on your back and pull your knees to your chest region.
  - Also, another stretch you can do is to lie flat on your back and make sure that your arms are stretched out in a "T" position. Then bend one knee and twist it in the direction of your straight leg while attempting to touch your bent knee to the floor (this is known as a spinal twist).

- You can also lie on your stomach and let your arms stretch overhead while lifting your chest as well as your legs off the floor. This is known as "superman."

- **Weight loss:** If you're battling with "baby weight," then it's possibly the cause of the lower back pain you're dealing with. You can refer how you can reduce "baby weight" earlier shared to help you reduce your weight. Your goal is to ensure that your weight falls within a healthy range for your height.

- **Use the proper footwear:** Another way to lower your risk of having lower back pain, increase stability, and improve your overall posture is to wear supportive footwear. But endeavor to wear footwears that are recommended for the kind of activity you're doing. For instance, you can wear snickers when you want to run or workout while boots are suitable for construction work. Well, putting on unsupportive shoes occasionally may not likely lead to lower back issues, but when you wear them for a prolonged time, you end up putting more pressure on your lower spine.

- **Quit Smoking:** One of the best things you can do for your new baby is to quit smoking. It's confirmed that smoking is a serious threat to our health. In fact, smokers stand a higher chance of suffering back pain than non-smokers. So, if you're smoking and also having baby weight, then chances are that you're having two possible causes of lower back pain. Nicotine which is found in cigarettes, restricts the flow of blood to the disks of your spine which makes them dry, crack and even rupture. Also, smoking leads to a reduction in the amount of oxygen in your blood and this further lowers the nourishment your muscles, as well as the tendons in your back, will get. Guess what? An unhealthy or weak back will be more vulnerable to strains or pulls, in addition to the symptoms of couvade syndrome. Giving up cigarette will not just help relieve you from back pain; it further enhances your health as you expect your baby.

- **When sitting, maintain the appropriate posture:** Another way to avoid having back pain is to maintain the proper posture whenever you're sitting. Ensure your feet is fixed on the floor if you have a desk job and make use of a chair that supports your lower back. Don't make it a habit of hunching forward while seeing your computer screen or while trying to use your keyboard.

- **Consider over-the-counter pain relievers (OTC):** Using OTC, especially the anti-inflammatory medications like ibuprofen, aspirin and naproxen can help reduce back pain or swelling. Depending on the extent of the pain, you may take them for several days based on the recommended dosage. But always bear in mind that these drugs aren't for everyone, so checking with your doctor before using any of them would be the best thing to do.

- **Massage:** Apart from stretching, massage is an excellent solution to your back pain because it helps to lengthen shortened muscles. Massage will also help to relieve most of the tension you have in your lower back. You can get a massage in addition to the stretches which we earlier discussed.

- **Get a better mattress:** Most people who experience lower back pain often benefit from sleeping on a medium-firm bed. But what would determine the kind of mattress you choose is your preferred sleeping position. For instance, side sleepers should go for a softer mattress to help them maintain good pressure while individuals who are back and stomach sleepers need a firmer mattress. It's recommended that you avoid sleeping on your stomach if you're having lower back pain.

Healthy Ways to Boost Libido

Based on the results of a particular study by US scientists, new mums may not have to be too worried that their partners are likely going to stray. This is because the results of the study suggest that new fathers are probably going to lose their sex drive. According to the study, during the first year of a new-born, new dads dropped a third of their testosterone while hands-on dads dropped a further 20 percent.

The researchers believe that the drop in the level of testosterone can help to mend relationships with issues, make fathers more caring, lower the chances of divorce and even make men "protective and less aggressive." According to the researchers at Notre Dame University, men, just like women during this period, would become more interested in protecting and caring for their offspring than anything else. In the words of one of the researchers, Dr. Lee Gettler:

"It's not just mothers who go through pregnancy and birth, and it's not just mothers who biologically respond to parenthood. "Our species has

evolved paternal instincts which are somewhat unique to our species compared with our closest relatives."

Another study also discovered that fathers with higher levels of testosterone have a lower tendency to take care of kids and give them attention and on the other hand, those with lower levels of testosterone displayed more sympathy as well as a greater desire to respond to their baby when they cry. While this appears to be good news for women, it's not completely the same for their male partners. This is because every man will always be concerned about their sex drive. Undoubtedly, a reduction in libido has been identified as one of the symptoms of couvade syndrome. But there are several ways expectant fathers can manage a possible decrease in their sex drive. We have been looking at various ways to handle some of the symptoms of couvade syndrome and in this section, we shall look at how you can enhance your sex drive, especially if it is one of the symptoms you may be having right now.

- **Eat Fruits and Aphrodisiacs:** Although there is not much (or strong) evidence to support the effectiveness of some foods, there is still no harm in trying. However, research suggests that eating certain vitamins can boost your sexual desire and performance. Apart from the fact that these fruits are believed to be aphrodisiacs, they are also among the best sources of essential minerals and vitamins. So, eating them will not only help to promote a healthy sex-life but will also help to increase blood flow to your genitals. examples of such fruits and other aphrodisiacs foods include:

- Avocados
- Figs
- Bananas
- Oysters
- Strawberries
- Pistachio nuts

Most of these foods that are believed to possess aphrodisiac properties have little scientific evidence to support how effective they are. However, some science-backed aphrodisiacs can help boost your libido. These natural alternatives are often preferred since they are safer with fewer side effects. Examples of such foods include:

- Red ginseng
- Maca
- Ginkgo biloba
- Saffron

- **Eat Chocolate:** Chocolate has always been loved by many, not just because they have a delicious taste, but also because they can enhance sexual pleasure. Results from a study revealed that the intake of chocolates helps to promote the release of phenylethylamine as well as serotonin into the body. This can lead to some mood-lifting and aphrodisiac effects. So, consider making chocolate one of your favorites to help you enhance your libido.

- **Meditation and plenty of sleep:** Stress is capable of affecting your sex drive negatively, especially with the increased level of stress while preparing for the birth of your baby. Stress and anxiety are some of the symptoms of couvade and if you're experiencing anxiety issues, then it may likely be the cause of your low sex drive. One of the ways to relieve stress is by practicing meditation. You can also take a yoga class or practice Tai chi. Considering the hectic and busy lifestyle most people have, it's most likely that you may not get the right amount of sleep. Taking care of your kids, wife and also going to work can further increase your stress level. But you can enhance your energy and sex drive by taking naps.

- **Reduce alcohol intake:** Taking two glasses of wine or more may be too much, especially when you're trying to boost your sex life. You can put your body at ease and even increase your interest in being intimate by taking just one glass of wine. But when you take too much alcohol, then you may lower your ability to perform well since it could affect your erectile function.

Chapter V

When you Don't Feel the Couvade Syndrome

While it's believed that a good number of men experience several symptoms of couvade, it's also possible that not all expectant fathers would experience it. Are you wondering why you're not experiencing any of the symptoms? Does it mean that you don't love your partner or baby enough? Do you think that something is wrong with you? Well, you shouldn't be worried at all because not all men will experience the symptoms of couvade. For instance, records show that the case of the syndrome in the United States is between 25-52 percent, 61 percent in Thailand, 20 percent in Sweden and estimates in the 1970s in the UK shows that between 11-50 percent of expectant dads have it. Generally, research results suggest that the incidence of couvade in western societies ranges from 11-67 percent, which actually suggests its legitimacy. So, it's possible that you're among those without the symptoms of couvade. But does it also imply that you may not be a good or caring father to your unborn baby? The answer is also NO! This is because even those who experience the symptoms may end up not being the best dads due to several factors such as unhealthy habits, lifestyle, wrong choices, and other environmental factors.

There is no proof that men who have couvade syndrome are better dads or that men without couvade are terrible partners and fathers. So, there is really no reason to be worried. Researchers are yet to determine the reason why some men fail to have the symptoms and they have also not identified if such cases lead to poor and undesirable outcomes. Does this imply that you're not predisposed to being a dad? The answer is NO! Your focus should be on being the best father to your baby and providing the best support to your partner. You may not have the symptoms of couvade; however, you may have your concerns regarding being a father, especially if you're a first-time dad. So, getting to know what to expect by going through the tips I earlier shared will help you prepare better and support your pregnant partner.

You have to make significant changes to your life as you await the arrival of your baby. Do you lack the right motivation to make the needed changes to your lifestyle? Well, the gift of life and entrance of your child into your home should serve as the right motivation to make the changes in your life. Being a father comes with a lot of responsibilities that are not meant to scare you, but it also comes with so much joy and fun. You don't have to focus on the challenges; instead, enjoy the fact that you're about to have a new member of your family who will always love you.

I believe that the tips and ideas shared in this book will help all fathers, whether you're having the symptoms or not. They can help you cut down your weight, get rid of stress and anxiety, plan better with your partner on how to give your baby the best and also help your partner with whatever challenges she may experience.

Conclusion

The truth is that pregnancy is a very crucial period for expectant dads as well as their partners. It's usually a time when they experience several physical symptoms which may appear as an expression or manifestation of deep psychological stress while they look forward to the birth of their child. So, as an expectant dad, you're likely going to also have this experience. Regardless of the origin of couvade - whether psychological or physical – one of the best ways to deal with the symptoms and overcome it is to be assured that you're not alone. Understanding that couvade syndrome truly exists and that many expectant dads in different locations around the world are experiencing it can be reassuring. Interestingly, most men who experience some of the symptoms mentioned in this book may not really talk much about it, but that does not imply that it's not common. In fact, the manifestation of most of these conditions may vary from complex to simple forms. In some cases, men may see it as normal health issues they face before while others may find it too strange to share publicly.

Perhaps one of the best things this information will do for you is that it helps you to deal with the fear of what is happening to you. For instance, a soon-to-be dad who wakes up to find himself experiencing morning sickness as well as other symptoms while his partner is pregnant may become frightened or confused. He may conclude that his symptoms may be as a result of some underlying health issues (which may be possible in some cases) and become worried.

The confusion and embarrassment of experiencing similar symptoms with his partner may prevent expectant fathers from even mentioning such issues to their doctor. So, when you're informed about couvade, you easily dismiss your embarrassment and worries. You understand what you may be going through and with the tips I also shared, you can easily cope with it without having to take medications. I would even advise that (depending on the intensity and frequency of your symptoms) you consult your doctor to be sure there are no underlying health issues.

One of the things that motivated me to write this book is that many expectant dads receive inadequate attention or concern for relieving the physical symptoms as well as their anxieties. Health professionals hardly ask about the well-being of soon-to-be dads – their psychological and physical well-being. This, in my opinion, is not the best approach. I believe that they should also be assessed. After assessing their needs, then interventions should also be suggested. Well, in the absence of such services, I firmly believe that with the information you've read in this book, you can overcome the symptoms you're having and be mentally prepared to have your child. Now, you can balance your needs, your partner's needs as well as your transition to fatherhood. I hope you got value from this book and I look forward to its impact in your life.

Thanks for reading! If you enjoyed this book or found it useful I'd be very grateful if you'd post a short review on Amazon. Your support really does make a difference and I read all the reviews personally so I can get your feedback and make this book even better.

Thanks again for your support!

References

BBC News. (June 14, 2007). Men suffer from phantom pregnancy. Retrieved on March 21, 2020, from http://news.bbc.co.uk/2/hi/health/6751709.stm

Balzen, J. (May, 2003). A Biological Perspective on Couvade: A Senior Thesis in General Studies. General Studies Council in the College of Arts and Sciences, Texas Tech University.

Brazier, Y. (February 16, 2018). What are pheromones and do humans have them? Retrieved on April 2, 2020, from https://www.medicalnewstoday.com/articles/232635

Brennan, A., Ayers, S., Ahmed, H. and Marshall-Lucette, S. (2007). A critical review of the Couvade syndrome: The pregnant male. Journal of Reproductive and Infant Psychology, 25(3), pp. 173-189. DOI: 10.1080/02646830701467207

Carey, E. (February 7, 2018). How to Stop Leg Muscle Cramps. Retrieved on April 4, 2020, from https://www.healthline.com/health/pain-relief/how-to-stop-leg-muscle-cramps

Cataldo, P. (n.d). Overcoming New Father Anxiety - Six Strategies to battle a Boss-Level Challenge. Retrieved on March 31, 2020, from https://daddymindtricks.com/new-father-anxiety/

Coleman, P. (August 16, 2016). Why Dads Gain Pregnancy Weight and How to Prevent It. Retrieved on March 31, 2020, from https://www.fatherly.com/health-science/dads-gain-pregnancy-weight-prevent/

Devi, A., & Chanu, M. (December 9, 2015). Couvade syndrome. International Journal of Nursing Education and Research. 3. 330. 10.5958/2454-2660.2015.00017.4. Retrieved on March 21, 2020, from https://www.researchgate.net/publication/283760127_Couvade_syndrome

Digestive WebMD. (February 14, 2019). Health Tips. Retrieved on April 3, 2020, from https://www.webmd.com/digestive-disorders/digestive-health-tips#1

Endley, B. (February 16, 2014). New dads lose sex drive as fatherhood reduces testosterone by a THIRD. Retrieved on April 6, 2020, from https://www.mirror.co.uk/news/technology-science/science/new-dads-lose-sex-drive-3152317

Frey, M. (September 21, 2019). How to Choose the Best Weight Loss Foods for Men. Retrieved on April 7, 2020, from https://www.verywellfit.com/the-best-weight-loss-foods-for-men-4129530

Ganapathy, T. (January, 2014). Couvade syndrome among 1st time expectant fathers. Retrieved on April 4, 2020, from https://www.researchgate.net/publication/269967353_Couvade_syndrome_among_1_st_time_expectant_fathers

Geddes, L. (March 12, 2014). How Does Pregnancy Affect Your Partner? Retrieved on April 6, 2020, from https://www.huffpost.com/entry/how-does-pregnancy-affect-your-partner_b_4949570?guccounter=1&guce_referrer=aHR0cHM6Ly93d3cuZ29vZ2xlLmNvbS8&guce_referrer_sig=AQAAAEuuoZ2eFARKu3Zd7I5jTe_wh-_01J2vkBear9FGEk6wH1G0B5i-v3RUUZs-4w7qEupYcGLrohTQVOT_56R5WsX_k8idt_Xd1WQcWGCxZzAVUanIsqOCUa5PepNW0IMObyG7Sp5G6H9nUcHBX180PmvnX3CwXjLgkjBmH6eYM3NK

Greenleaf, R. (March 11, 2020). 10 Tips for Dealing with Lower Back Pain. Retrieved on April 4, 2020, from https://www.virtua.org/articles/10-tips-for-dealing-with-lower-back-pain

Groves, M. (July 4, 2018). The 11 Best Ways to Improve Your Digestion Naturally. Retrieved on April 3, 2020, from https://www.healthline.com/nutrition/ways-to-improve-digestion

Health.com. (March 4, 2014). 15 Everyday Habits to Boost Your Libido. Retrieved on April 6, 2020, from https://time.com/12090/15-everyday-habits-to-boost-your-libido/

Healthline. (July 28, 2016). 10 Daily Habits to Stop Back Pain. Retrieved on April 4, 2020, from https://www.healthline.com/health/back-pain-management#stop-smoking

Kendall, K., and Smith, C. (April 25, 2019). The Complete Guide to Losing Weight. Retrieved on March 31, 2020, from https://www.bodybuilding.com/content/the-complete-guide-to-losing-weight.html

Kingston University London. (June 23, 2010). Lecturer investigates hormonal link to 'sympathy pregnancies' in men. Retrieved on March 22, 2020, from https://www.kingston.ac.uk/news/article/171/23-jun-2010-lecturer-investigates-hormonal-link-to-sympathy-pregnancies-in-men/

Lambert, C. (October 17, 2011). Better memory, bigger tum and lower sex drive - how being a dad changes men. Retrieved on April 6, 2020, from https://www.dailymail.co.uk/health/article-2050216/Better-memory-bigger-tum-lower-sex-drive--dad-changes-men.html

Mayo Clinic. (n.d). New dad: Tips to help manage stress. Retrieved on March 31, 2020, from https://www.mayoclinic.org/healthy-lifestyle/infant-and-toddler-health/in-depth/new-dad/art-20045880

Mayo Clinic. (n.d). Muscle cramp> Retrieved on April 4, 2020, from https://www.mayoclinic.org/diseases-conditions/muscle-cramp/diagnosis-treatment/drc-20350825

McCoy, K. (August 24, 2017). 10 Tips for Better Digestive Health. Retrieved on April 3, 2020, from https://www.everydayhealth.com/digestive-health/tips-for-better-digestive-health/

Men's Fitness Magazine. (May 16, 2019). The Men's Fitness Definitive Guide to Fat-Loss. Retrieved on March 31, 2020, from https://mensfitnessmagazine.com.au/the-mf-guide-to-fat-loss/

NHS. (April 12, 2019). 8 tips for healthy eating. Retrieved on March 31, 2020, from https://www.nhs.uk/live-well/eat-well/eight-tips-for-healthy-eating/

Parker, W. (November 21, 2019). The Fears of Dads-To-Be and How to Address Them. Retrieved on March 31, 2020, from https://www.liveabout.com/fears-of-dads-to-be-1270767

Patel, A. (May 13, 2013). Weight Loss Men: 10 Ways for Dads to Lose 'Baby Weight.' Retrieved on March 31, 2020, from https://www.huffingtonpost.ca/2013/05/13/weight-loss-men-exercises-_n_3252875.html

Petre, A. (June 28, 2017). 7 Aphrodisiac Foods That Boost Your Libido. Retrieved on April 6, 2020, from https://www.healthline.com/nutrition/aphrodisiac-foods

Razzaque, W. A. A., Husain, K., and others. (March 2008). False Pregnancy in Bitch, Division of Animal Reproduction, Gynecology and Obstetrics. Veterinary World, Vol.1 (3): 92-95

Scott, E. (March 06, 2020). How to Practice Basic Meditation for Stress Management. Retrieved on April 7, 2020, from https://www.verywellmind.com/practice-basic-meditation-for-stress-management-3144789

Severson, A. (April 17, 2017). Boost Your Libido with These 10 Natural Tips> Retrieved on April 6, 2020, from https://www.healthline.com/health/boost-your-libido-10-natural-tips

Smith, C. M. (n.d). Lifehack Presents: A Mini-Guide for Weight Loss for Men. Retrieved on April 7, 2020, from https://www.lifehack.org/articles/lifestyle/lifehack-presents-a-mini-guide-for-weight-loss-for-men.html

Smithson, A. (September 4, 2014). 5 Fears of Becoming a Dad; and How to Kick the Fear to the Curb. Retrieved on April 4, 2020, from http://truparenting.net/5-fears-becoming-dad-kick-fear-curb/

Trimble, T. (November 05, 2019). Couvade Syndrome: The Curious Cases of Men Who Get Pregnancy Symptoms. Retrieved on March 21, from https://www.fatherly.com/health-science/couvade-syndrome-men-pregnancy-symptoms/

Vince, G. (February 1, 2006). Dads-to-be pile on the pounds too. Retrieved on March 21, 2020, from https://www.newscientist.com/article/dn8661-dads-to-be-pile-on-the-pounds-too/

WebMD. (March 21, 2003). Advice for Expectant Fathers. Retrieved on March 31, 2020, from https://www.webmd.com/men/features/advice-for-expectant-fathers#1

What to Expect. (August 17, 2018). 6 Surprising Pregnancy Symptoms — for Dads! Retrieved on March 21, 2020, from https://www.whattoexpect.com/pregnancy/photo-gallery/surprising-pregnancy-symptoms-for-dads.aspx

122

About the author

Patrick A. **Simon** is the author of four amazing books and has been exploring the world of writing since 2017. Born in the early '80s, P. A. Simon embraced pedagogy as a major field of study though he still devotes his time to other areas of study, especially economics. Being a dad and having a master's degree in pedagogy, he has acquired extensive experiences throughout his life, which serves as inspiration for his books. This has also helped him to effectively communicate and connect with his readers by writing in a light and straightforward tone that people can easily read and understand.

He loves writing about topics related to paternity, budgeting and personal management. His first book *"Soon to be DAD: Handbook For Expectant Fathers"* explores pregnancy from a male perspective. He wrote the book mainly for expectant dads who appear to be ignored during their significant other's pregnancy to help them understand the kind of experiences they will be having. The book provides an account of his experience with his wife's pregnancy and provides tips and advice to help readers who may be going through a similar situation. As a continuation of the first book, he published his second informative book, *"Couvade Syndrome: What Male Sympathetic Pregnancy is & how you can Fight it."* While the first one focused mainly on what soon-to-be dads should expect when their partner gets pregnant, the second one took it a step further. It focused on why soon-to-be fathers are having the strange pregnancy symptoms they may be sharing with their pregnant partners.

Another field of interest that P. A. Simon explores through his writing is family budgeting and personal money management. Based on his experiences in life as an involved father and husband, as well as his profound understanding of economics, especially budgeting, he has also devoted significant attention to household budgeting. His short e-book *"Family budgeting: Guide to Managing Household Finance"* was written to help families make the best use of the money they have, and ensure proper management of their finances without major hiccups due to overspending.

P. A. Simon just finished his fourth book on personal finance (*"How to Manage Money When You're Not Earning Enough"*) which provides excellent tips for individuals with low income to help them manage their finances effectively. Although he is not a professional in this field, his extensive experience with money management, both in times of crisis and abundance, has prepared him for many money-related disasters. He hopes to help his readers to be prepared as well. These delightful books are fun to read and come right from the heart of someone who has experienced all of these things first-hand. They are his perspective on various aspects of family and parenthood, which would help his readers understand their familial commitments better and be in the best position to fulfill their responsibilities. Undoubtedly, the books are a true family necessity!

Apart from writing, Simon is a father who passionately devotes his free time to his son, cooking, engaging in physical activities (he loves running and plays volleyball in an amateur league), and acquiring more knowledge in the field of economy and child psychology.